T0380807

CRACKING THE ROCK

Implementing organizational change in the Rockwell Corporation

Warrington S. Parker Jr, Ph.D

BALBOA.PRESS
A DIVISION OF HAY HOUSE

Balboa Press books may be ordered through booksellers or by contacting:

Balboa Press
A Division of Hay House
1663 Liberty Drive
Bloomington, IN 47403
www.balboapress.com
844-682-1282

Print information available on the last page.

ISBN: 979-8-7652-5560-5 (sc)
ISBN: 979-8-7652-5559-9 (e)

Balboa Press rev. date: 10/07/2024

CONTENTS

FOREWORD

I wrote a book about my personal life titled Strength of Will, published in January 2024 on Amazon. This current book focuses on my professional life. It was written to explore and understand why I was effective as an internal organizational psychologist and change agent at Rockwell, despite not being originally hired for that role. While working at Rockwell, I never paused to analyze why I was effective; I simply continued doing what worked, relying on my education, experiences, intuitive sense, social skills, and change agent abilities. This approach allowed me the opportunity to realize my vision of organizational change.

DEDICATIONS

This book is dedicated to my parents, Warrington S. Parker, Sr., and Pauline M. Dais Parker, both of whom have passed on. It is also dedicated to my lovely wife, Brenda A. Cunningham Parker, affectionately known as Gigie. She has been a steadfast source of support throughout every move our family made during my time at Rockwell. Her unwavering encouragement and assistance have been invaluable. Thank you. These important individuals have inspired and motivated me to write this book. As a proud note we have been married for 61 years, with four children and four grandchildren.

ACKNOWLEDGMENTS

My wife, Brenda Ann Cunningham Parker, known as Gigie, was especially encouraging. She loved listening to my stories and consistently urged me to put them in written form. While composing this work, she was a tremendous help in refining the manuscripts of all the chapters. Our four children were also exceptionally encouraging and supportive throughout my experiences, traveling almost every month, and during this incredible writing journey.

- **Warrington S. Parker III**: A Partner in the law firm of Crowell & Moring, San Francisco.
- **Shanga Kyle Parker**: An actor who had roles in TV series like *The Fresh Prince of Bel-Air* and *All in the Family,* and a full professor at NYU, an adjunct professor at Columbia University, and an adjunct professor at the Iceland University of the Arts in Iceland.
- **Monique Lynette Parker Huffins**: An educator and a health-oriented retailer.
- **Kala Nakeba Parker**: A Pediatrician.

They all understood that I would often be on business trips and yet would return to attend events they wanted me to be at—basketball, baseball games, cross-country races, field trips, lacrosse games, and father-daughter dances.

I also want to mention an important person in my life who first introduced me to organizational change: Dr. Floyd Mann, Director of the Institute for Social Research (ISR) and the Center for Research on the Utilization of Scientific Knowledge (CRUSK) at the University of Michigan, Ann Arbor. He was a family friend and mentor who hired me and supported my position at the University. He also guided me in completing my Ph.D. in Organizational Psychology.

Additionally, I want to acknowledge several external Rockwell consultants who assisted me in implementing large-scale organizational change at Rockwell: Paul Hulbert, Dave Miller and Associates, Mike Marker, and Bob McDermott.

INTRODUCTION

As an organizational psychologist, my focus has been on studying job design, workplace productivity, employee satisfaction/commitment, management, and leadership styles. My primary interest lies in large-scale organizational strategic change strategies, employee involvement in workplace changes, the social-psychological needs of employees at work and the benefits of team-based work environments.

The path that led me to this field is complex. Growing up in Jim Crow-era Mobile, Alabama, perhaps inspired a desire to address societal injustices and empower individuals in shaping policies that affect their lives in the workplace. Both the academic study and Ph.D. training, along with the practical application of organizational psychology, felt natural and effortless to me, especially in promoting business performance and employee involvement in organizational change.

I wrote this book to gain a deeper understanding of why I was effective as an internal organizational psychologist and change agent at Rockwell. As I mentioned, even though I was not hired to be an internal change agent. I aimed to uncover the factors contributing to my effectiveness in driving organizational change and improving workplace dynamics. The experience was unique, as I was the first African American hired in this role at Rockwell. This made me question whether my effectiveness was influenced by my identity or the strategies and principles I implemented. I also wrote this book to hopefully impart insight to those interested in pursuing a career in Organizational Psychology, interested in organizational change.

Through writing, I realized that possessing theoretical knowledge and academic training alone isn't enough for real impact. Despite being well-trained at the University of Michigan, I found that effective change management requires both science and art. Intrapersonal, interpersonal and other social skills, like emotional intelligences, are crucial, as is the ability to connect with people, understand company culture deeply, and intuitively apply scientific theories.

In hindsight, blending the science and art of organizational psychology seemed to come naturally to me. I believe my effectiveness was not significantly impacted by my race; rather, the combination of the science and art.

This book is designed for those seeking an in-depth understanding of the pivotal role an internal organizational change agent plays within a large enterprise. It is particularly valuable for those looking to master the complexities of executing extensive organizational strategic transformations. Executives, managers navigating substantial changes, organizational change consultants, educators, and students specializing in Organizational Psychology will find this book indispensable.

In this book, I will discuss the principles and strategies that governed my work as an organizational change agent. I will explain how I combined the science and art of being an internal organizational psychologist and change agent, as well as the strategies I implemented to overcome organizational resistance to change. I have also included business results from implementing large-scale organizational "Fit" change strategies in Rockwell businesses. Along with several accounts of the outcomes of these changes in various divisions and operations, including Coralville, Iowa Operations; the Semi-Conductors Division in Newport Beach, CA; the Automotive Business, Troy, Michigan; Rocketdyne Division in Canoga Park, CA; Collins Business in Cedar Rapids, Iowa; and Bellflower High School in Bellflower, CA.

Additionally, I will describe the process of change implemented during Rockwell's Union-Management Master Contract Negotiations, where we used a "Win-Win, Building Trust While Negotiating" process. I played a role in designing and implementing this process, earning trust from both sides, and using my social and change agent skills to ensure adherence to the process, blending both science and art. Next I will discuss why I was ready to leave the University of Michigan for a position in industry.

CHAPTER 1
READY TO LEAVE THE ACADEMIC WORLD

In 1977, after six fulfilling years as a professor at the University of Michigan Dearborn, Michigan, campus, School of Management, I felt it was time to transition from academia to industry. I wanted to apply what I had been teaching to business students and implement the concepts of organizational change I had learned during my experiences and in the PhD program. Despite the high risks associated with such a move, I was confident in my ability to succeed in a performance-based environment outside the academic sphere—a position where pay was based on performance, not dependent on the state budget. Some of my college colleagues were doubtful, but I was ready to take on the challenge.

The decision was one of high risk and potential high reward, but I was willing to take the leap. Later, while working at Rockwell, I sent those doubting colleagues an article from *Industry Week Magazine* titled "The Bold New Rockwell World," which highlighted my effectiveness in the company. The article is included later in the book.

I often pondered with my wife, "Should I leave the academic world and move to industry?" I knew that academics making the transition to industry might have to accept a more junior position initially. However, before joining Rockwell, I had already developed teaching skills at the university and gained experience in organizational change, which helped me progress quickly once I made the move. My academic knowledge of organizational change, change agent skills, and ability to connect with executives were crucial. Additionally, I applied my social skills and strategies to overcome resistance to change, drawing on my prior experiences in organizational and community change.

I also had a vision of organizational change that I wanted to realize when I transitioned from the University of Michigan to industry. This vision, developed before joining Rockwell, drove my desire to fundamentally improve the structure, systems, and processes of organizations by involving the people affected by the change. I also aimed to design organizations that addressed the socio-psychological needs of employees, which were often missing from the traditional assembly-line model in the U.S.

Rockwell's decision to develop Executive Leadership Development Programs in 1977 for its top 200 executives presented a unique opportunity for me. Additionally, the experience of my undergraduate and master's degree business students returning to tell me about their impressive salaries after graduation made me reevaluate my own situation. I wanted a job that paid based on performance, like in business, and I was willing to take the risk. To be honest, I didn't fully know what I didn't know, but I was confident that I would figure it out.

I was hired into the Rockwell Automotive Business as a manager of training and leadership development for top executives. Although I was not hired specifically as an internal organizational change agent, I was determined to find a way to realize my vision and achieve my goals from this position. I had to figure it out, and I knew that I would.

———————————————◦◦◦◄●►◦◦◦———————————————

CHAPTER II
WHY ROCKWELL?

When I decided to leave academia, I had no clear idea which organization I would join. Serendipitously, a headhunter contacted me about a job at Rockwell Automotive just as I was seeking employment in industry. Several factors contributed to my decision:

- **Tenure and Career Ambition**: I was up for tenure at the university but was eager to enter the emerging global competitive marketplace to apply my knowledge of organizational change. My goal was to make a significant impact by fundamentally improving the structure, systems, and processes of organizations while also considering the socio-psychological needs of employees.
- **Desire for Performance-Based Compensation**: Unlike academia, where salaries are often state-controlled, I wanted a job where compensation was based on performance. This desire stemmed from hearing about the impressive earnings of former students who had entered the business world.
- **Rockwell's Leadership Development Initiatives**: In 1977, Rockwell's leadership began developing executive developing programs for their top 200 senior executives. In 1978, I was hired into the Automotive business to design and implement executive leadership development programs for the top executives and managers.

I pondered over the decision to leave academia for industry, aware that it was a high-risk, potentially high reward move. My belief that I could advance rapidly in the industry was rooted in my expertise as a change agent and my experience in both organizational and community change efforts. The move, though uncommon at the time, proved to be highly rewarding.

Before joining Rockwell Automotive, one of Rockwell's business sectors, I had a vision, purpose, and goals for organizational change. These were shaped by my experiences and understanding of the global competitive business environment. I was determined to realize my vision and achieve my goals, focusing on transformational changes that reshape business strategies, structures, systems and processes. My commitment to change management persisted despite the challenges, driven by the belief that organizational stagnation leads to regression.

I had been influenced by my early interest, reading and studying of the Hawthorne Effect before joining Rockwell. I studied the Hawthorne Effect, which describes a change in an individual's behavior resulting from their awareness of being observed. The effect suggests that workers tend to alter their behavior at work in response to the attention they receive from their supervisors. I found out it required more than observations.

The Hawthorne Effect derives its name from industrial experiments carried out in Chicago's Hawthorne suburb (now called Cicero) in the 1920s and 1930s. The research comprised several productivity studies that tested the impact of changes in lighting and work structures, such as break times and working hours, on employee productivity.

Later interpretations by different researchers revealed that being the subject of a study and receiving increased attention from researchers can result in a temporary improvement in worker productivity. However, a 2009 experiment by the University of Chicago suggested that the original study's results were likely overstated. Written by the CFI Team.

Also, early in my college days at St. Procopius College in Lisle. Il, I studied Sociology and was influenced by reading *The Organization Man,* Whyte, who stated his central thesis, which was that the American organizations—and especially the large corporations—were systematically stamping out individuality, for collective behavior and that people were foolishly allowing this to happen. That this loss of individuality would eventually be ruinous to both the individual and the corporation. I did not find this to happen. I found that no corporation would argue that conformity is better than individuality. I have found that no corporation believes it anymore.

CHAPTER III
HISTORY

The Rockwell Corporation and the Rockwell Automotive Business

Understanding the history of an organization is crucial for its employees and those working in the organization. This knowledge can foster a sense of pride and purpose, beyond merely earning a paycheck or working to bring about change. As Socrates said, "The secret of change is to focus all of your energy not on fighting the old, but on building the new." Rockwell Corporation, a major American high-technology corporation, exemplified this ethos. It was involved in various sectors, including the Automotive Business, Aircraft and Space industry (notably in building the BIB bomber, space shuttle and its main engines), Avionics (Commercial and Defense), Automation, and Commercial and Defense Electronics. The company has a rich history:

- **Founding and Growth**: The predecessor to Rockwell Manufacturing Company was founded in 1919 by Willard Rockwell. By 1968, it had seven operating divisions manufacturing various products, including industrial valves, power tools, automotive truck axles and automotive parts, and gas and water meters. The Automotive, originated in 1909 and became known for manufacturing heavy-duty truck axles and drivetrains, as well as power windows, seats, and locks.
- In 1973, it was renamed Rockwell International after merging with North American Aviation an aerospace business.
- **Expansion and Diversification**: The diversified technology company employed approximately 120,000 people at its peak, serving customers in aerospace, defense, automotive, telecommunications, avionics, and more.
- **Significant Acquisitions and Innovations**: In 1985, Rockwell International acquired Allen-Bradley, an Automation company, marking it the largest acquisition in Wisconsin history at the time.

Each sector comprised multiple divisions and manufacturing plants. As an Organizational Psychologist and change agent for Rockwell, I had the opportunity to work across all these sectors, starting in the Automotive business.

I started my experiences in the Rockwell Automotive Business, as the manager of training and executive leadership development for the top 50 executives and for managers. After joining the Automotive business, I soon realized based on my organizational change experiences in organizations training of managers, team building of managers with their direct reports would not transform organizations when there was a need to do so.

Before joining Rockwell Automotive, I had a purpose, vision, and goals about what I wanted to realize and achieve in initiating change in organizations. The vision and goals were formed because of experiences trying to change organizations. In the manager training position, I was determined to find ways in the Automotive business to realize my vision and achieve my goals.

The vision and goals were to fundamentally change organizations, transformational changes. Changes that completely reshape the structure, tasks, and processes that would redefine a business. My interest was also in organizing organizations, that included the socio-psychological needs of employees in the workplace. These are dramatic, large-scale strategic changes strategies that fundamentally alter organizations.

Going from Manager of Training in Rockwell To An Internal Organizational Change Agent to Realize my Vision

When I joined the Rockwell Automotive business, it was confronting an increasingly competitive global marketplace, as well as the challenge of emerging high-technology industries, in ways never experienced before. As the Manager of Training and Executive Leadership Development, I believed the company needed more than just training for managers and executives to thrive in this new global landscape.

My vision, upon joining the Automotive Business, was to fundamentally transform the organization by implementing large-scale organizational strategic change initiatives. These initiatives would bring about significant and comprehensive changes across the company's entire system—its goals, strategies, structure, tasks, reward systems, processes, employee skills, and culture. I was determined to involve the entire workforce in the change process, ensuring the new design promoted high employee performance, motivation, and a deep commitment to both the organization's goals and their own personal growth. Visions are powerful, and I was driven by one I was determined to realize.

However, I was uncertain whether I could accomplish my vision, goals, or purpose of organizational change from my role in training. From my experience, training managers, leaders, and team-building alone would not be enough to achieve the scale of change I envisioned. I took a risk, knowing that if Rockwell's leadership did not align with my vision, it could put me in a precarious position.

This is how I added the role of Internal Organizational Change Agent to my responsibilities in management training within the Automotive Business. My interest in becoming an internal change agent stemmed from experiences before joining the organization. Training managers and building management teams alone did not align with the vision I had for transforming organizations. To gain deeper insights and enhance my ability to drive transformational change, I enrolled in the Ph.D. program at the University of Michigan.

During my Ph.D. program, I studied Socio-Technical Systems Theory, an organizational design theory. I learned that socio-technical theory views any work system as composed of both social and technical subsystems, with the objective of optimizing both for overall system success. I also explored the works of Dr. R. Walton on innovative work systems and high-performance systems, an emerging new form of organizational design. In addition, I studied Dr. Michael Beer's concept of high-performance organizations and Dr. Lou Davis' work on innovative work systems.

I found these ideas compelling and believed that if I could apply this type of organizational design at Rockwell, it would significantly contribute to realizing my vision.

I reached out to Dick Walton to ask who could help me learn the design process that could lead to this new organizational form. Without hesitation, he recommended Paul Hulbert, an organizational consultant with experience designing similar systems at Procter & Gamble and TRW, an aerospace company. I contacted Paul, and together we worked to design two new plant startups: one in Asheville, NC, and the other in York, SC. Both startups were successful, and that success solidified my new role as an internal organizational change agent. In doing so, I met a critical need for Rockwell, one they had not fully realized.

After 25 years at Rockwell, I retired, having served in two capacities: as an internal organizational change agent and continuing my work in Management and Executive Leadership Development.

The risk I took worked. But I am not sure how I was able to start the design process of the two new plants. I knew this design process could lead to the realization of my vision.

And it did.

CHAPTER IV
PROMOTION TO THE CORPORATE OFFICES. PITTSBURGH. PA

"I know the price of success: dedication, hard work, and an unremitting devotion to the things you want to see happen."

—Frank Lloyd Wright

In 1980, I transitioned to the corporate offices of Rockwell promoted to the Corporate Director of Organizational and Executive Leadership Development, later advancing to Vice President. My hard work and passion for the job were recognized as I climbed the organizational ladder, moving from Manager to Director, and eventually to Vice President.

The corporate offices were the heart of Rockwell, providing strategic support and guidance to the entire business globally. These offices played a crucial role in supporting all other facilities and were integral to Rockwell's worldwide operations, which were organized into Strategic Business Units and Business Divisions. Although I was invited to remain in the Automotive Business and promised a Vice Presidency there, I chose to move to the corporate offices to have worldwide responsibilities in diverse businesses.

In my corporate role, I continued implementing large-scale strategic organizational change strategies and designed world-class leadership development programs for the top 200 executives and managers globally. I also developed Functional Executive Leadership Development programs, fostering teamwork across various functions, including Engineering, Manufacturing, and Human Resources. At Rockwell Collins in Cedar Rapids, Iowa, I developed leadership programs for the top 100 executives and managers worldwide and collaborated with the President of Collins to redesign the $3.5 billion business.

Organizational Change Accounts

A report or description of an event or experience: "a detailed account of what has been achieved"

Rockwell's success stories in implementing large-scale organizational change strategies were documented and used as teaching tools in Executive Leadership Development programs focused on organizational change. These accounts were taught by the business President or General Manager who led the change on the multi-level design teams.

For my work in developing the Rockwell Executive Leadership Development Programs, I was honored with the Peter F. Drucker Distinguished Speakers Award. "Video recording of a presentation by Warrington Parker, Ph.D. for the Drucker Distinguished Speakers Series, titled "The Transformation of Rockwell: A Leadership Development Agenda." Parker discusses changes at Rockwell International as it scaled down from 120,000 employees to 46,000 and sold its aerospace and defense businesses to concentrate on electronics and communication. According to Parker, leadership involves innovation, creating new business opportunities, and creating a culture of continuous learning. He goes on to discuss the four constituents whose judgement Rockwell values: customers, employees, shareowners, and the community. Parker also discusses different types of Rockwell leadership learning programs, an employee survey conducted every 18 months, and the core values of the company." *https://ccdl.claremont.edu/digital/collection/dac/id/7759.*

An Account of a Redesign Project of a Division, (1B$,10,000 Employees

One notable account discussed, is a project with Rocketdyne's President, who requested my assistance in redesigning the Space Shuttle Main Engine (SSME) Division. After attending a Rockwell executive development program that discussed one of the Accounts about organizational change. We formed a cross-functional design team consisting of 35 members, including the President, Vice Presidents, government funding customers, union leaders, members and rank-and -file employees. I always asked to include on the design team several employees who were doubting Thomas's. If they started to support what the design team was doing, I knew I was making progress.

A year after completing the design process, a Ph.D. student, Molly K. Smith-Olsson, conducted a quasi-longitudinal pre-test/post-test study at Rocketdyne for her dissertation. The study measured changes in employee perceptions about the organization during significant change and was conducted in 1991.

Results Achieved:

- **Cost Reduction**: The cost of the SSME was reduced by 25%.
- **Production Efficiency**: Rocketdyne produced seven engines instead of five, with 1,000 fewer employees.
- **Quality Improvement**: The lowest material review defect rate in history was achieved, along with improved cycle time across nearly all product areas.
- **Customer Satisfaction**: Rocketdyne received the highest customer rating, leading to one of the highest award fees.

Outcomes of the Redesign:

According to interviews conducted by Anthony Velocci (1991) with managers at Rocketdyne, several successes were attributed to the Socio-Technical Systems (STS) redesign. For example, workers devised a new method of inspecting manufactured components, identifying defects as the component was produced, which eliminated the need for post-production quality inspections. Additionally, defects were reduced by 50%, directly impacting cycle time.

These early results mirrored those reported by other organizations that had undergone an STS redesign process

A Caution Was Raised by the Chief Engineer of the SSME

In the middle of the design process the Chief Engineer of the Space Shuttle Main Engine, pulled me aside and said Dr. Parker if you keep going with this design process you are going to kill a lot of people. Startled, surprised and got concerned for a few minutes I responded, I will not stop the design process. After completing the design process and implementation was on-going thank the heavens, I was right. **A summary of the study is included in** *Appendix B.*

CHAPTER V
THE NEED TO CHANGE — NEW ORGANIZATIONAL MODELS

In the early 1960s and 1970s, the intensifying global business environment I believed necessitated large-scale organizational changes, in organizations, moving beyond incremental adjustments, like I had learned in Organizational Development (OD). Implementing such changes was challenging, particularly for businesses with a history of success.

With the organization's success I had to find a way to overcome resistance to change. It would be crucial, for success. Implementing organizational change was akin to changing tires on a vehicle speeding down a highway—organizations needed to continue performing, not missing a beat, while undergoing transformation. I was interested in sharing different organizational models that were emerging, that were different then the assemble-line bureaucratic models American model.

New Organizational Models

The traditional command-and-control, bureaucratic models were becoming outdated and left customers dissatisfied. I believed a new organizational paradigm was needed for the 1980s and beyond. As Galbraith & Lawler II (1993) noted, shifting from highly functional vertical structures to lateral or horizontal organizations could provide better integration and coordination, essential for gaining a competitive advantage. Ostroff (1999), further emphasized that the traditional vertical model was inadequate for the modern competitive, technological, and workforce environment.

This old model, influenced by the division of labor and scientific management principles from Frederick Taylor and Adam Smith, focused on efficiency and productivity through highly specialized roles. However, this structure was not conducive to the demands of the emerging global market and the emerging of knowledge workers.

Personal Experience and the Role of Organizational Psychology in Organizational Change

My early experience working on an assembly line at a Ford Motor plant exposed me to the limitations of rigid, non-thinking jobs. This experience, along with my work on organizational change projects at the ISR Institute for Social Research at General Motors, spurred my interest in understanding and implementing effective organizational change. I relied heavily on my intuitive sense of change, but I soon realized my limitations. I mentioned this to Dr. Floyd Mann, the Director of the ISR, Center for the Utilization of Scientific Knowledge (CRUSK), who hired me to work on the ISR-GM change project. With Floyd's support, I enrolled in the University of Michigan's Organizational Psychology Ph.D. program.

I pursued a Ph.D. and master's in Psychology, in Organizational Psychology to learn more about organizational change, focusing on optimizing business performance and employees' well-being. I was interested in applying what I learned about systems of organizational change, which involves applying psychological principles to large-scale organizational change processes to redesign the American historical assembly-line organization. These changes improved work environments, including communication, employee commitments, satisfaction, and safety. My goal was to inspire and lead planned changes in the workplace, increasing employee satisfaction, commitment, organizational efficiency, and achieving business goals.

Influences That Increased My Interest in Organizational Change

Before joining Rockwell, my interest in organizational change was influenced by the research on team-based high-performance, high-commitment organizations by Dr. Walton, Dr. Michael Beer, and Dr. Lou Davis. These scholars emphasized the Socio-Technical Systems (STS) design process, which integrates the technical and social aspects of work to optimize both. I aimed to transform Rockwell organizations into this model, knowing it would benefit both the business and its employees. I also knew I had to influenced senior executives that my goal was consistence with my vision. If not, I would have to change or leave the company.

Contrasting Organizational Forms

I studied the differences between traditional U.S. assembly-line organizations and innovative, team-based high-performance organizations. The latter, as described by Dr. Walton, emphasized self-managing teams, broad job roles, and employee commitment to employee development. These organizations showed high levels of employee satisfaction, low turnover, and impressive economic performance. I realized I had to learn the design process to achieve this new innovative organizational design. Dr. Walton from Harvard Business School recommended Paul Hulbert, a consultant retired from Procter & Gamble Company, to assist in this process.

High-Performance Organizations vs. Traditional Models

High-Performance Organizations (HPOs) and team-based designs are characterized by:

- Achieving sustained growth, outperforming their peers over at least five years.
- The ability to adapt quickly to changes.
- A long-term orientation.
- Integrated management processes where strategy, structure, processes, and people are aligned throughout the organization.
- A focus on continuously improving and reinventing core capabilities.
- Significant effort spent on developing the workforce.
- A team-based organizational design that implicitly considers the social-psychological needs of employees, including eliminating or minimizing "we-they" issues that cause status differences among employees.

High-Performance Organizations are more flexible, and customer-focused, allowing for greater innovation and responsiveness. The following definition of an HPO is proposed: A High-Performance Organization is an organization that achieves financial results better than its peer group over a longer period by adapting well to changes, reacting quickly, managing for the long term, setting up an integrated and aligned management structure, continuously improving its core capabilities, and truly treating its employees as its main asset. This definition is based on research by Waal, A.A. de (2005), "The Foundations of Nirvana: The Characteristics of a High-Performance Organization," white paper, *www.andredewaal.nl.*

In contrast, traditional models are often internally driven, rigid, and focused on control rather than empowerment. The assembly line, a foundational concept in manufacturing, represents a production process that breaks down the creation of a product into a series of sequential steps, each performed by a different worker or machine. Ford's assembly line was revolutionary because it significantly reduced the time and labor required to produce a car. This efficiency allowed Ford to lower the price of his cars, making them affordable to the average consumer. The success of Ford's assembly line led to its adoption across various industries, transforming the manufacturing landscape and influencing the school system and most U.S. organizations (Mingo, 7777 Bonhomme Ave, Suite 1800, Clayton, MO 63105, *(Info@MingoSmartFactory.com).*

Implementing these high-performance models required careful planning and the involvement of all organizational levels. It was essential to integrate both the technical and social systems to elicit high commitment from employees and increased business performance. The success of these changes often depended on the support and active involvement of leadership.

In summary, my experiences in organizational change highlighted the importance of transitioning to models that emphasize team-based structures, employee empowerment, and continuous learning. These elements are crucial for organizations to remain competitive in a rapidly evolving global market. The comparison between traditional and high-performance organizations provided a roadmap for the changes needed at Rockwell, guiding my efforts to implement large-scale strategic organizational transformation processes.

CHAPTER VI
GOVERNING CHANGE PRINCIPLES AND STRATEGIES

As an organizational change agent, I adhered to key principles and implemented strategies that ensured the effectiveness of change initiatives at Rockwell. These were rooted first in my intuitive sense of organizational change, my experiences, social skills and my academic training in the field.

1. **Know the Business and the Need for Change**: Understanding the business, the case for change, the culture, rationale behind the necessary changes, and the competitive environment were crucial. This knowledge allowed me to craft relevant and impactful change strategies that aligned with the company's goals and market realities.

2. **Personal Connections with Business Leaders**: Building trust with business leaders was essential. I conducted face-to-face interviews to gather information and establish rapport, which facilitated the development of leadership programs tailored to their needs. Sharing personal experiences and finding common ground helped in establishing strong, trust-based relationships. Especially needed when you come out an academic position with a Ph.D.

3. **Forming a Design Team for Organizational Change**: A design team was vital in guiding the change process. This team included a diverse group of stakeholders—business leaders, managers, hourly employees, and union representatives. For government-funded businesses, customer representatives were also included. This inclusive approach ensured that all perspectives were considered, fostering buy-in and reducing resistance.

4. **Engaging Employees and Addressing Resistance**: Involving those affected by changes in the design process was key to overcoming resistance. Addressing the question, "What's in it for me?" and engaging employees in the process helped to minimize resistance. Dissatisfaction with the status quo often makes people more open to change.

5. **Implementing and Sustaining Change**: Drawing from Kurt Lewin's Change Model—Unfreeze, Change, Refreeze. I focused on unfreezing existing structures, implementing new strategies, and then solidifying these changes within the organization's culture with an

implementation plan. This approach embedded changes and ensured they were sustained over time. When a business completes the design process you do not click a switch and WOW the change happens, it requires an implementation plan.

My work at Rockwell was guided by these principles, which helped achieve effective and lasting change. The process of organizational change is challenging, requiring robust leadership and a deep understanding of both technical and social systems. My goal was to design organizations that inherently elicited high performance, motivation, and commitment from employees, aligning both organizational business and individual goals.

———————————◄●►———————————

CHAPTER VII
CONNECTING TO TOP EXECUTIVES TO INFLUENCE

Connecting with executives through face-to-face interviews was a key strategy I used to overcome resistance to organizational change at Rockwell Automotive and at the corporate level. Face-to-face communication is often the most impactful, as it allows us to truly "see" one another and be fully present. Clara Capano, a master instructor, and coach, "emphasizes the importance of leading with service to others," and this approach guided my interactions. Before introducing large-scale organizational change strategies, I aimed to connect personally with the executives I needed to influence through direct, in-person interactions.

I began in the Automotive business, by identifying individual leadership development plans for the top 25 executives in the business. After conducting desk audits of their personal histories, I met each executive in their offices—a place where they felt comfortable behind their desk. During these interviews, I gathered information about their educational and personal development needs. I asked them to share their backgrounds, educational experiences, and the influences that shaped who they are today. In return, I shared my own experiences, focusing on areas of commonality, such as shared values or similar upbringings. This process not only provided valuable information for their development plans but also helped them get to know me personally.

Another way I connected with the top executives was through internal executive development programs conducted off-site. Attending these sessions with them allowed me to know them outside of their offices. We shared meals, dressed casually, and engaged in informal conversations, all of which contributed to building strong relationships. These interactions increased my ability to influence the executives, regardless of race, as they got to know me better. I believe that when we take the time to know each other personally, we can better appreciate our differences and similarities.

To Be Heard, I Listened

Overcoming the stereotype of a College Professor was essential. I was told that I had Black board "chalk on the back of their coat." In the industry, this phrase often described someone who pontificates theories without practical application. I realized that to convey knowledge about organizational change effectively, I needed to adapt my language to resonate with the executives. By integrating theoretical knowledge with industry-specific language and practical insights, I was able to communicate more effectively and gain their trust.

Applying Change Agent Skills

In hindsight, I applied a set of change agent skills that proved invaluable in my role as an internal change agent in Rockwell. While I wasn't formally trained in these skills, they became instrumental in overcoming resistance to organizational change and earning the trust of Rockwell executives. These skills included:

- **Emotional Intelligence**: The ability to read and understand others' emotions and manage my own.
- **Self-Awareness**: Understanding my strengths, weaknesses, and motivations, biases, which allowed me to be more effective in my role.
- **Modeling Behavior**: Demonstrating the change I wanted to see, which helped build credibility.
- **Strategic Thinking**: Applying a systems approach to problem-solving, recognizing that there are multiple ways to achieve a goal. The principal of Equifinality.
- **Intuition**: Trusting my gut feelings and using them to guide decision-making, a skill that often led to positive outcomes.
- **Expressing Truth to Power**: Being willing to challenge existing practices and propose solutions, even when it was difficult.
- **Building Strong Relationships**: Establishing trust and rapport with executives through personal connections and shared experiences.

These skills, combined with a clear vision and commitment to change, allowed me to drive significant organizational transformations at Rockwell. My success was not only due to the strategies I implemented but also to the relationships I built and the trust I earned from those I worked with.

CHAPTER VIII
FORMING DESIGN TEAMS TO FOLLOW A DESIGN PROCESS

"Behind every genius is a team," says Murphy. Working as a team leverages diverse perspectives, skills, and experiences to find creative and effective solutions to complex problems. Team members learn from each other and can avoid costly mistakes. A crucial component of implementing effective change at Rockwell was forming a diverse design team guided by a facilitator. This team included individuals from all levels of the organization, ensuring that the perspectives and needs of all stakeholders were represented.

In my work, I often asked the business leader to form a design team consisting of 20-30 members, including the business leader, senior executives, managers, rank-and-file employees, and union leaders. Teamwork encourages smarter risk-taking. While working alone might lead to hesitation in taking risks, in a team, there is collective support that encourages bold steps, which can lead to groundbreaking ideas.

Albert Einstein is often credited with discovering the theory of relativity, but he relied heavily on conversations with friends and colleagues to refine his concept. This collaborative approach is common in innovative environments. As noted by Atlassian, "When people play off each other's skills and knowledge, they can create solutions that are better than one function."

Involving employees directly in the change process is crucial for several reasons:

1. **Increased Buy-in and Ownership**: When employees are involved in decision-making, they are more likely to understand, accept, and commit to the changes.
2. **Enhanced Productivity and Flexibility**: Employee participation often leads to greater engagement, which can boost productivity. It also fosters a more adaptable workforce that is open to new ideas and approaches.
3. **Improved Communication and Morale**: Effective communication is critical in change management. Involving employees helps ensure that the rationale behind changes is clearly understood, reducing stress and improving morale.

4. **Stronger Relationships and Reduced Stress**: Involving employees in the change process can lead to healthier relationships between staff and management, as well as reduced stress levels.

5. **Boosted Morale and Commitment**: Change is never easy, and people often resist it because they are unsure about the future or the outcomes of the proposed changes. No one wants to leave their comfort zone and take on new roles and responsibilities. However, when they are actively engaged in the change process and involved in decision-making, they start to feel more positive about the change and their new roles. This engagement boosts their morale and commitment to the change.

By understanding and applying these principles, I effectively led and supported the implementation of large-scale organizational change strategies at Rockwell.

CHAPTER IX
DESCRIPTION OF CHANGE STRATEGIES IMPLEMENTED IN ROCKWELL

In Rockwell, I spearheaded the implementation of comprehensive organizational change strategies, with external change agents to collaboration to accelerate the process. I initially led these change initiatives within the business units, strategically transitioning the management of the design process to external consultants when the timing was right. Notably, only one business leader explicitly requested, me to lead the change process. I want you to lead the design process." I accepted this challenge for the Rocketdyne Division, the builder of the Space Shuttle Main Engine—a billion-dollar enterprise employing 10,000 people. This design effort is referenced later in the book.

These organizational change initiatives aimed to maintain a competitive edge, improve operational efficiency, and enhance profitability while prioritizing employee well-being. The strategies were multifaceted, addressing both the technical and social dimensions of the organization to achieve optimal results. These were proactive, large-scale organizational change processes, implemented well before the businesses faced potential failure.

> "Change before you have to." — Jack Welch, former CEO of General Electric.
> "Slowness to change usually means fear of the new." — Philip Crosby
> "People don't resist change. They resist being changed!" — Peter Senge
> "Change is hard because people overestimate the value of what they have." I experienced them all.

Large-Scale Organizational Strategic Change Strategies

What are they, and why did I choose to implement them?

I led the implementation of large-scale organizational strategic change strategies to help businesses transform their core design and functioning. The objective was to stay ahead of the competition, enhance efficiency, and increase profitability while improving employee well-being. Change is essential to remain relevant and foster innovation, and transformational change is critical. John Kotter of Harvard Business School argues that around 70% of major change efforts fail, often because organizations do not take the holistic, systems-based, long-term approach needed to see change through successfully. This holistic, systems-based approach was a strategy I consistently applied.

Driven by the evolving global competitive marketplace, I recognized the need for large-scale strategic organizational change strategies at Rockwell as early as 1978, even before Kotter's book on change. The large-scale change processes I implemented focused on redesigning or optimizing the core business processes—those that create and deliver value to customers and drive the company's revenue stream.

Large-scale change strategy is a systems approach to organizational transformation. It helps organizations improve the alignment between various design components (e.g., goals, strategy, tasks, structure, processes, technology, behavior, decision-making) and employee participation, while considering the socio-psychological needs of employees.

A description----Allan M. Mohrman Jr. and Susan Albers Mohrman, among others, describe large-scale organizational change as transformational, contrasting with traditional change, which is typically incremental. Lawler (1989) characterizes large-scale change as a process that results in lasting transformation of an organization's character, significantly altering its performance. Nadler and Tushman (1989) agree, noting that large-scale change affects the entire organization, is pervasive, and involves fundamental, frame-breaking, or paradigm shifts.

Blake and Mouton (1988) also describe this type of deep organizational change as transformational, in contrast to the more gradual, incremental nature of traditional change. In a rapidly changing global environment, organizations like Rockwell face complex issues affecting various strategic functions. The regulatory landscape, competition, employee attitudes, and resistance to change are among the daily challenges. Globalization and increased migration patterns add to the pressures businesses face, thereby heightening the demand for strategic solutions that enhance effectiveness.

In the 1970s, companies like Rockwell increasingly recognized the urgent need to respond to a changing global environment. Senior leadership understood the importance of being agile, adaptive, and willing to change, though some were uncertain about how to proceed.

I guided Rockwell's business leaders through a successful change process using design teams. I introduced Whole Systems Transformation (WST), a comprehensive approach required to transform businesses. Drawing from the business environment, best practices, and integrated theories, WST enabled organizations to achieve faster, more cost-effective, and sustainable positive change.

As David Bradford highlighted in the last edition of *Practicing OD*, Whole Systems Transformation (with "whole" being the operative word) facilitates change that is all-encompassing and addresses the issues of the entire organization. (*Power Up: Transforming Organizations Through Shared Leadership*, first published February 1, 1999.)

CHAPTER X
WHOLE SYSTEMS TRANSFORMATION (WST)

Whole Systems Transformation (WST) was the approach I utilized in organizational change efforts, which necessitates the modification of all parts of the system. WST transforms the organization into a "unified whole," shifting it from its existing configuration to an entirely new one.

WST fundamentally differs from the conventional view of organizational development, which typically involves understanding and modifying existing systems according to a predetermined plan to achieve successful change. In contrast, WST recognizes the inherent need for change and advocates for an approach that reinvents the organization itself. This process is not merely about transforming all the systems within the organization; it's about creating an entirely new system.

In the following sections, I will explore the implementation of large-scale organizational change strategies, with accounts and provide insights into overcoming resistance to change.

CHAPTER XI
IMPLEMENTING LARGE-SCALE ORGANIZATIONAL CHANGE STRATEGIES

Strategic Organizational Change "Fit" Models

The concept of "fit" is central to modern organizational design and was a key focus in the process of change within Rockwell. This systems approach suggests that an organization's design must align with its strategy and other contingency factors. Organizations that achieve this alignment tend to deliver better financial performance, while a misfit can lead to disorganization and, consequently, lower performance (Schlevogt, 2002). The better the alignment of the organization's key components, the stronger the business performance and the improved well-being of employees.

> *"Organizational change has a considerable psychological impact on the minds of employees. To the fearful, it is threatening because it means that things may get worse. To the hopeful, it is encouraging because things may get better. To the confident, it is inspiring because the challenge exists to make things better."*
>
> — King Whitney Jr.

> *"In life, change is inevitable. In business, change is vital."*
>
> — Warren G. Bennis

> *"Change cannot be put on people. The best way to instill change is to do it with them. Create it with them."*
>
> —Lisa Bodell.

Socio-Technical Systems Design Process A Large-Scale Organizational Change Strategy

The goal is to achieve the best possible relationship and fit between the technical and social systems, considering the social and psychological needs of employees., while striking the balance to optimizes both the technical and social aspects of the organization.

| SOCIAL | TECHNICAL |

- INFORMATION FLOW
- MORALE/ATITUDE
- PEOPLE SKILLS
- ORG. STUCTURE
- RELATIONSHIPS BETWEEN GROUPS
- JOINT OPTIMAZTION

- HARDWARE
- EQUIPMENT
- POLICIES
- PROCESSES
- LAYOUT/SPACE

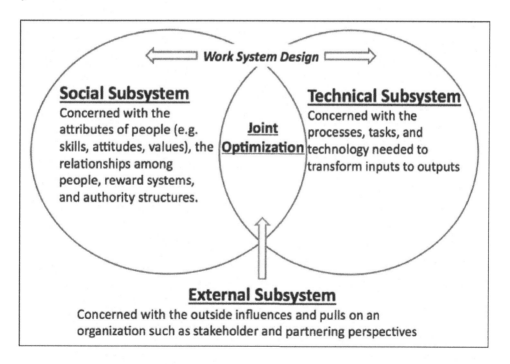

Technical Definition

Organizational technology encompasses the sum of man-made contrivances or developed processes that alter, refine, or create new goods and services delivered by organizations. This includes electronics, software, documents, new techniques, or any combination thereof used in the delivery of services. Even in highly automated systems, human involvement is essential for the technical system to function effectively.

The Human Organization

A Human Organization is more than just a place to earn a paycheck; it is a space where individuals engage in deeply fulfilling work that matters. It is an environment that educates and transforms, where individuals evolve into not only competent managers but also inspiring leaders. This is a place that fully harnesses the potential of its team members, fosters rich, collaborative relationships, and leverages disagreement for growth rather than avoiding it. Here, individuals have the autonomy to make decisions essential for great work, with access to the information necessary to make those decisions. The goal in my organizational change work at Rockwell was to optimize both the technical and social systems—the human system.

My Role in Change Management

My interest in change management was one of the most challenging aspects of my leadership and role as a change agent. It required me to gain the trust of business leaders, inspire teams and executives to overcome their resistance, and maintain the momentum necessary to guide the organization to success. Overcoming resistance to change was often critical, as the process of organizational change can be likened to changing tires on a truck while it's moving down the highway— and it must be changing while continuing to perform. The pressure to manage change while maintaining performance rested heavily on business leaders, who were integral members of the design teams participating in the change process.

Design Teams

I implemented and supported large-scale organizational change strategies through design teams, which typically consisted of 20-30 members from across the business, including senior executives, managers, rank-and-file employees, and union leadership. In my work with the Graphic business in Chicago, IL, we utilized a design team of 50 members. Despite its size, this team was both effective and manageable.

One of the first organizational change strategies implemented was the Socio-Technical Systems Design process in the Automotive Manufacturing Business. All change strategies considered the business environment, the voice of the customer, the structure of the manufacturing plant and the socio-psychological needs of the employees at work.

CHAPTER XII
THE SOCIO-TECHNICAL SYSTEMS DESIGN

For Manufacturing Organizations

Manufacturing organizations are typically characterized by assembly lines where products move along a fixed path, and workers perform specific tasks at each station. These organizations transform raw materials into finished products by utilizing assembly lines, prioritizing quality control, managing supply chains, and focusing on cost management and reducing lead time. Continuous improvement is crucial for their success.

At its core, the socio-technical systems design asserts that the design and performance of any organizational system can only be understood and improved when both the 'social' and 'technical' aspects are integrated and treated as interdependent parts of a complex system. This approach emphasizes the importance of considering the socio-psychological needs of employees—needs that were often overlooked in the traditional assembly-line organizations of the early 1900s, such as those managed by Henry Ford and Frederick Taylor.

Sharon Beder, notes that Henry Ford, like Taylor, had a rather low opinion of workers on his assembly lines: "The average worker, "I am sorry to say, wants a job in which he does not have to think. Those who have what might be called the creative type of mind and who thoroughly abhor monotony are apt to imagine that all other minds are similarly restless and, therefore, to extend quite unwanted sympathy to the laboring man who day in and day outperforms almost the same operation." Today knowledge works are in the workforce. 'Much of what today's knowledge workers encounter daily seems unprecedented and unfamiliar. However, the wisdom of Peter Drucker, the "father of modern management," remains timeless and applicable to today's challenges in business and other organizations. Drucker coined the term" knowledge workers" in the late 1950s, before it was obvious that there were many such people in the world. I believed that Rockwell organizations were hiring knowledge workers and no longer employees from the farm workers who had a problem reading and writing. Rockwell manufacturing organizations were hiring knowledge workers who responded differently to the workplace.

In the following sections, I will present accounts of Rockwell businesses that implemented large-scale organizational strategic change strategies.

CHAPTER XIII
AN ACCOUNT OF THE ROCKWELL COLLINS BUSINESS, CEDAR RAPIDS, IOWA

The *Socio-Technical Systems Design Process*

Rockwell Collins was a $3.5 billion aviation defense and commercial electronics business employing 14,500 people worldwide, headquartered in Cedar Rapids, Iowa. The company was highly successful, with an annual growth rate of 11% over the past three years. To further enhance its success, the President and senior team developed a vision, strategic goals, objectives, and an overall Collins strategy: optimize the core business (revenue value stream), expand the core, reduce costs, and achieve operational excellence through implementing the Socio-Technical Systems organizational design process.

When I joined Rockwell Collins, customers were demanding that their suppliers reduce costs, improve efficiency, enhance product quality, reduce waste, and speed up product delivery. With the support of the President of Collins, I began implementing the Socio-Technical Systems Design Process, which led to the creation of a high-performance, highly committed organization. This process was aimed at responding to customer demands. I was supported by David Miller and Associates Mike Marker and Bob McDermott in this effort. We were in the process of implementing the Socio-Technical Design process when customers began requesting their suppliers to implement Lean Manufacturing Principles to meet their demands. In response to this, the President renamed the design process to the Lean Electronics process. The Lean Principles and the Socio-Technical Systems design process had similar design outcomes.

Collins achieved the following goals:

- 50% reduction in cycle times and inventories
- 35% increase in productivity
- 30% reduction in costs
- 25% reduction in floor space

The next large-scale organizational change strategy was implemented in knowledge-based organizations like Rockwell Divisions, which do not produce tangible products like manufacturing plants.

McKenzie 7'S and Jay Gilbreath's Strategic Change Frameworks

I modified the change frameworks to focus on the alignment of the organization's goals, strategy, structure, systems, tasks, processes, culture, and employee skills. This framework was implemented in divisions of $500 million to $1 billion businesses. One division that implemented this change process was the Semiconductor Division, which is described later in this account.

I used the model as an organizational analysis tool to assess and monitor changes within the internal situation of an organization with a design team. This process was implemented with a team consisting of the President of the division, his direct reports, and a cross-functional team responsible for the success of the business, including union members. The model served as an assessment tool for the design team, and after analysis, it was used to identify when these organizational parts were not in alignment. The design team would then recommend changes to achieve alignment.

At one point, a divisional president resisted the implementation of the framework, doubting that rank-and-file employees had any insight into what was needed to improve the division. He was proven wrong.

Nonlinear Design Process for Knowledge-Based Organizations

A nonlinear organization is one that does not form a straight line, like a manufacturing organization such as an automotive plant. A nonlinear system is one in which the change in output is not proportional to the change in input.

I implemented a nonlinear change process in Rockwell's Engineering, R&D, Rockwell's Space Wars project, and Human Resources organizations. I also applied the nonlinear design process to redesign the Hum an Resources Organization at Rockwell Collins, working with Bill Richter, Vice President of Human Resources. This nonlinear design process was described and discussed in a book written by a professor from Case Western Reserve University Business School in Cleveland, Ohio. After reading the book, I was able to successfully implement the process in Rockwell's engineering and R&D organizations, Space War technology, and human resources organizations.

To implement these change strategies, it was crucial to develop strategies to overcome resistance to organizational change, as change can be challenging even when it is ultimately beneficial.

CHAPTER XIV
STRATEGIES TO OVERCOME RESISTANCE TO ORGANIZATIONAL CHANGE

I worked to overcome resistance to organizational change in Rockwell. It was important to understand and identify resistance issues as well as those who supported the change. Any level of change can cause resistance, whether it be a new team member joining, an employee leaving, or a major organizational shift through strategic change strategies. It is human nature to be concerned about change, and I respected that concern by involving those affected in the strategic change strategies. I often heard the question, "What's in it for me?" The more I could answer that, the more open people were to support the change. However, I also found that sometimes, even when employees knew the change would be beneficial, they would still resist.

I mentioned that it was possible to change an organization when there is a high level of dissatisfaction, usually due to a lack of business success. The greater the pain and dissatisfaction with the status quo, the more open people were to supporting change. I learned that organizational and personal change often starts with some form of pain, such as dissatisfaction with business performance. I also used Kurt Lewin's information to assist me.

Kurt Lew in Change Model

Kurt Lewin's Change Model involves three steps: Unfreeze the Organization (Make the Case for Change), Change the Organization, and Freeze the Changes (Refreeze). Lewin is recognized as the "founder of social psychology," which highlights his interest in the human aspect of change. I studied his change model, taking social psychology courses in my PhD program. I would recommend to business leaders that they inform their organizations why change was necessary by making a compelling case for change to unfreeze the organization. Then, they would indicate that the organization was going to go through a change process that would benefit the organization.

Building Trust and Overcoming Resistance

I found it crucial to connect with senior executives that I needed to influence. Face-to-face interviews were important for building trust and overcoming resistance to organizational change. The most impactful communication always happens face-to-face. When we connect in person, we "see" one another and can be more present.

I started by identifying individual executive leadership plans for each executive and for the group. I began with interviews after completing a desk audit of their personal history on file. After the desk audits, I interviewed each top executive, meeting them in their offices, a place of comfort for them. These interviews were conducted to collect information about their educational and/or other personal development needs.

During these personal interviews, I asked them to share their background, educational experiences, who they were today, and who or what had influenced them most in becoming who they were, starting from any age they were comfortable with. Afterward, I did the same, focusing on areas of commonality, such as whether they grew up Catholic, were altar boys, or grew up in a poor family. I was making a connection. I realized that when a new person enters a room, others in the room probably want to know who that person is. This connecting interview process helped me gather information for developing their executive educational plans and helped them get to know me personally.

Another way I got to know the top executives in the business was by developing internal executive development programs conducted off-site and attending the sessions with them. I got to know them outside of their offices; we ate together, dressed casually, drank wine together at dinner, and even went to the men's bathroom together. All these experiences were bonding opportunities. These interactions increased my ability to influence the executives, regardless of race, as they got to know me better. I believe that getting to know each other personally and sharing different and similar experiences can help us value our differences. I believe we are more similar than different. I was surprised to learn that Ph.D.'s had to overcome chalk on the back of their suit coats.

Applying Change Agent Skills

I focused on the principle of Equifinality, which suggests that there is no one way to achieve a goal (i.e., there is more than one way to skin a cat). I wanted executives to see that there are multiple ways to achieve organizational goals beyond the traditional assembly line concept.

An organization can set goals, develop strategies to achieve the goals and I wanted them to know that there are several ways to achieve them. There may not be one best way. In the leadership development programs, I shared several different organizational forms, comparing them to the assembly-line model, so executives could see that there were other organizational structures that could compete with the one they were managing.

This concept applies to everything from problem-solving to achieving business success. It can be applied at various levels of complexity. It's important to keep this principle in mind when trying to achieve goals because it means that there is more than one way of doing so—you have options beyond just one solution to a problem. I also believe that the set of change agent skills I learned and applied at Rockwell assisted me in overcoming resistance to change.

In hindsight, I applied a set of change agent skills that proved useful in my role as an effective internal change agent at Rockwell. I was neither personally nor professionally trained in these skills before applying them, but I believe they helped me overcome resistance to organizational change and build trust with Rockwell executives, demonstrating through my actions that I knew what I was doing.

- **Knowing others is intelligence:** This involves the ability to read others using emotional intelligence.
- **Knowing yourself is true wisdom:** Having intrapersonal skills allows for deep self-awareness.
- **Mastering yourself is true power:** As Lao Tzu and Brian Tracy suggest, self-mastery is a powerful skill.
- **Using myself as an instrument of change:** I trusted my intuitive sense—often referred to as "gut feelings." Intuition tends to arise holistically and quickly without conscious awareness of the underlying mental processes. Scientists have repeatedly demonstrated how information can register in the brain without conscious awareness and positively influence decision-making and other behaviors (*Psychology Today*).
- **Modeling behavior as a consultant:** Part of my role as an internal and external change agent was to model change behavior. As Mike Marker, an external change agent I worked with, observed, "You have done this everywhere I have seen you."
- **Belief in the change strategies, coupled with leadership skills:** To be a successful change agent, I needed to believe in and be convinced of the change strategies I implemented. This required patience, flexibility, and strong social persuasive skills.
- **Systems thinking and strategic communication:** I was a systems thinker, a strategic thinker, and a person who could confidently communicate. I also had to assure the general managers that they would not lose control of their business during the change process.
- **Knowing yourself, being confident, and self-assured:** I learned to know myself through several personal development labs. This was sometimes a painful journey, as it involved discovering who I am as a human being and how others see me. The journey was unpredictable and deeply engaging, bringing me face-to-face with my deepest fears,

self-doubts, vulnerabilities, and insecurities. Knowing oneself means understanding one's strengths and weaknesses, passions and fears, desires, and dreams. It also means being aware of one's eccentricities and idiosyncrasies.

- **Calling out "garbage" when dysfunctional behavior occurs in the design process:** I developed the ability to address dysfunctional behavior directly when it occurred.
- **Expressing truth to power:** I worked on challenging and improving existing practices, proposing solutions for problems I identified, and collaborating with colleagues to implement those solutions. I recently learned that civil rights leader Bayard Rustin coined this term.
- **Developing ideas and working with executives:** As a change agent, I worked with executives, presenting specific ideas about new forms of organizations. When an executive agreed to lead or support the change design process, I proceeded to implement the organizational design process. I realized that these skills were important for success in life and as a change agent.

It was helped to be confident and self-assured, starting with the love I received from my mother and father, reinforced by the love of relatives and positive feedback from work. I had trust in my abilities, qualities, and judgment, which was related to love, experiences, and education. Getting to know myself was a journey that I did not purposely pursue.

Following is a discussion about the importance of executives "seeing is believing and believing is seeing" in business results from the redesign change processes.

———————————◦◦◦◄●►◦◦◦———————————

CHAPTER XV
BUSINESS RESULTS

Seeing is Believing, and Believing is Seeing Can Be Motivating

The business results from various Rockwell Businesses that completed the Socio-Technical Systems design process were significant. This design process was implemented across the corporation, including in new manufacturing plant startups and the redesign of traditionally structured organizations, even those with union representation. The process was also effectively applied in divisions ranging from $300 million to $500 million, as well as in billion-dollar businesses, encompassing up to 10,000 employees. These outcomes were often highlighted in Rockwell's Executive Leadership Development Programs, demonstrating the effectiveness of the approach through the achievements of their peers.

During my tenure in organizational change, I did not encounter anyone else in the field who had applied this design approach as comprehensively across divisions, billion-dollar businesses, or educational institutions using the Socio-Technical Systems design process—notably, beyond Rockwell organizations.

The strategies and principles outlined above were instrumental in driving successful organizational change at Rockwell. By focusing on both technical and social systems, integrating science and art, involving all stakeholders, and employing a range of change management skills, I was able to lead and support significant transformations within the company. This approach not only improved organizational performance but also fostered a more positive and engaged workforce.

Success in business is not accidental; it results from strategic decisions, persistent efforts, and a steadfast commitment to achieving results. I gained support for my change initiatives at Rockwell by presenting tangible business outcomes from the implementation of large-scale organizational change strategies. The positive results from two new plant startups were shared with senior executives, showcasing the effectiveness of the Socio-Technical Systems design process, which I implemented with the assistance of Paul Hulbert, an external organizational change agent.

The Ability to Persuade and Influence Executives

In organizational change, the ability to persuade and influence senior executives is crucial. These skills can foster trust and garner the necessary support for implementing change. Brian Tracy, a renowned authority on sales training and personal success, emphasizes that learning to persuade and influence others is key to achieving personal power and success. This capability allows individuals to leverage their skills and abilities at the highest level, earning the respect and support of customers, colleagues, and superiors. Next, I will present another account of a Rockwell business.

CHAPTER XVI
AN ACCOUNT OF ROCKWELL AUTOMOTIVE BUSINESS

My experience in designing educational leadership development programs for top executives in the automotive industry was instrumental in paving the way for large-scale organizational strategies. These programs were critical in opening doors for further change initiatives when I was promoted to the corporate offices.

The Automotive Workshop for Senior Business Leaders

The implementation of an educational organizational change workshop for senior executives in the automotive sector proved to be a pivotal moment. The workshop, coordinated by Dr. Richard Walton of Harvard Business School and other experts, introduced the top 25 executives to various organizational structures and theories, such as High-Performance-High Commitment organizations, Theory Z, and the Scanlon reward pay system. This educational approach served as a medium and agent of change, providing the executives with insights into innovative organizational designs that could lead to improved effectiveness and productivity.

The workshop's success was evident when the automotive president encouraged the executives to innovate and develop improvement plans for their respective business units. This endorsement allowed me to apply the high-performance organization planning and design process to two new automotive plant start-ups in Asheville, North Carolina, and York, South Carolina.

The Startup of Two New Automotive Manufacturing Plants

With the assistance of Paul Hulbert, an external organizational consultant from Procter & Gamble—a leading company in starting up new plants using this design process—we worked together to implement the organizational design process for two manufacturing plants: the York,

South Carolina, front axle plant, and the Asheville, North Carolina, rear axle plant. These plants experienced the most successful start-ups that the automotive division had ever seen.

In 1983, the York plant achieved direct labor efficiency of 92% using a 100% standards program, with only two job classifications for a 350-person plant. The plant operated under an all-salaried concept and became a leader in the automotive industry for inventory turns. As of 1984, the York plant achieved 18.0 inventory turns, compared to an automotive average of 5.0 turns. The cost of capital savings associated with these improved turns was $80,000 per year, and the plant received the Ford Q1 award in 1983.

The Asheville facility became profitable just six months after start-up. Customer delivery credibility remained over 99% for one year, sales volume was 24.7% above plan, and profit before tax was 9.3 times the plan. The facility operated with only three job classifications and maintained an all-salaried concept, with no time clocks, no reserved parking spaces (first come, best spaces), and no separate cafeteria for managers. The goal was to design an egalitarian, high-performance organization.

Next, I will discuss the origins of the Socio-Technical Systems Design Process that I have implemented.

CHAPTER XVII
ORIGINS OF THE SOCIO-TECHNICAL SYSTEMS DESIGN PROCESS

The socio-technical systems approach, developed by the Tavistock Institute in the UK, emphasizes the joint optimization of both social and technical systems within an organization. This approach has proven effective in improving performance by aligning the needs of both the organization's social and technical systems.

The Design Phases: The Socio-Technical System Design Process Implemented at Rockwell

The design process, learned from Paul Hulbert and supported by external consultants, involved forming a design team representing all stakeholders. This two-week process aimed to optimize the core business processes and supporting systems. The principles guiding this process included focusing on customer and environmental needs, empowering autonomous units, and ensuring minimal interdependence among work units.

The results of these efforts were tangible, as evidenced by the successful start-ups of the new plants and the overall improvement in organizational effectiveness. This success highlights the importance of a well-executed change strategy, supported by education, persuasion, and the right mix of social and technical system optimization. The success of these two plants paved the way for my role as an internal organizational change agent, a role that continued to be impactful following my promotion to the corporate level.

Next, I will provide a detailed account of the use of this approach in the organization and what has been achieved in implementing large-scale organizational change strategies.

CHAPTER XVIII
ACCOUNT OF THE ROCKWELL CORALVILLE, IOWA OPERATION

Implementing the Socio-Technical Systems Design Process

This account delves into the implementation of the Socio-Technical Systems Design Process at Rockwell Collins' Coralville, Iowa Manufacturing Operations. The primary goal was to optimize both social and technical systems simultaneously. The phases of this process were carefully followed, and the resulting outcomes were documented.

A design team, comprising the Plant Manager, all levels of managers, hourly employees, union leaders, and members, was formed to navigate the design process. The Rockwell account, among others, served as a valuable teaching tool in Rockwell's Executive Leadership Programs.

The Value of Using Real-World Accounts in Leadership Development Programs

These accounts were specifically tailored for use in Rockwell's Leadership Development Programs as teaching aids on organizational change. They provided several key benefits:

- **Real-World Examples:** They offered executives tangible examples of large-scale organizational change processes and results, demonstrating that if their peers could achieve success, they could too.
- **Discussion Opportunities:** They gave executives the opportunity to discuss a real-world Rockwell example of organizational change.

All accounts were specifically tailored for use as educational aids in Rockwell's Leadership Development Programs on organizational change

CHAPTER XIX
ACCOUNT OF THE DESIGN PHRASES OF THE ROCKWELL CORALVILLE. IOWA OPERATION

This account was specifically designed for Rockwell's Leadership Development Programs, with the Plant Manager leading the discussions. The organizational planning and design process at Coralville unfolded in seven phases, involving nine facilitated sessions from early January to mid-June of 1986. The plant started operations with only the management team, gradually expanding to over 400 employees within two years.

The process began with the Plant Manager and Director of Production Operations, emphasizing the need for innovative approaches to maximize plant goals and objectives. The team was charged with implementing and managing the designed processes, focusing on achieving superior production, quality, cost reduction, and employee participation.

Coralville's Plant Manager highlighted the need for a systematic approach, noting the initial challenges faced by the plant team. The facility was unique within Rockwell for involving union (IBEW) negotiations before starting operations, leading to a cooperative and simplified work contract designed to enhance flexibility.

Coralville met its manufacturing, productivity, and quality targets while expanding to employ over 400 workers. The plant achieved full production, implemented a new MRP II Production Inventory System, and was instrumental in the development of high-tech GPS equipment. The Plant Manager credited the rapid start-up and success to the new organizational planning and design process.

In 1994 and 1995, *Industry Week Magazine* recognized the Coralville operation as one of the "Best 25 Plants" in the United States, and in 1996, it was named one of the "Best 10 Plants" in North America.

Phases of the Socio-Technical Systems Design Process Implemented at Coralville

1. **Business Givens:** Senior management set mandatory goals, which were uncompromisable and essential for the plant's success.
2. **Individual Needs Goals:** These goals were designed to enhance employee motivation and commitment, encompassing aspects like challenging work, job satisfaction, clear responsibilities, and competitive compensation.
3. **Productive Purpose Statement:** A technical analysis detailing the core processes from raw material input to product output.
4. **Environmental Needs Analysis:** Identified objectives to effectively interact with external entities, such as customers and government agencies.
5. **Mission or Charter:** Defined the organization's purpose, serving as a guiding principle during the design process.
6. **We-They Analysis:** Focused on eliminating status differences within the organization.

Design Phases:

- **Phase I: Goal Setting:** Establishes foundational goals and individual needs for the organization.
- **Phase II: Analysis and Core Process Design:** Develops a detailed technical task analysis and sets up the core manufacturing process.
- **Phase III: Staff Support and Management Organization Design:** Defines the support and management structure required for the new organization.
- **Phase IV: Administrative Systems Design:** Designs systems to support the manufacturing and management components.
- **Phase V: Pay and Progression Systems:** Recommends systems for pay, progression, and rewards based on performance.
- **Phase VI: Transition Strategies:** Assists the organization in transitioning from start-up to full operation.
- **Phase VII: The Renewal Process:** Ensures the organization continually assesses and adapts its operations to maintain high performance.

This structured approach ensured that the Coralville facility not only met its initial targets but also became a model of high-performance operation within Rockwell.

There was another article in *Industry Week written* about my change work *"Rockwell's Bold New World"*

By DONALD B. THOMPSON

he "D. R. Beall" to whom the above memo is addressed is Donald R. Beall, Rockwell International Corp.'s 48-year-old president and chief operating officer. And you can rest assured that when he writes, "I hope we are communicating with GMs," the general managers are being communicated with.

This is no "read, file, and forget" exercise.

Rockwell is far down the road in redesigning itself into one of the "future organizations" that Mr. Beall and his associates believe are the best hope for being competitive.

What is taking shape at Rockwell is, in fact, as far removed from the traditional corporation as the company's B-1B bomber is from the buggy whip.

"How we organize ourselves and manage—and how we incorporate the whole subject of employee participation and involvement—is funda-

mental. It's just damned necessary competitively," Mr. Beall declares.

THE OPEN SECRET. The simple fact is that companies using new organizational design elements are outperforming traditional organizations by 30% to 40% in all business measurements, says Dr. Warrington S. Parker Jr., Rockwell's director of organization and executive development.

That gets known among people involved in organizational design, Dr. Parker confides, even though most such firms (Cummins Engine, Procter & Gamble, and Exxon, among

Parker "... High commitment by employees is presumed in the basic design of the organization."

are fostering now with the total employee group on the realities of the market, the competition, and the results of the business, to get a true understanding of the real situation."

As administrator, so to speak, of the Rockwell "change," Mr. Murphy is clear on the requirement to remain competitive: "If you're not willing to risk a fundamental and integrated organizational change based on a deliberate questioning of every element of doing business, you're wasting your time," he says.

Dr. Parker elaborates: "Many companies recognize the competitive breakdown. They take a piecemeal approach to fixing it—the classic moves of a motivational program, quality circles, buying a [better] piece of equipment. American industry is faddish. [It's] looking for a silver bullet, a quick fix.

"American companies can't survive tinkering that way. But to transform an organization—now that's a big order. What unlocks the organizational mind, the worker potential?"

What indeed?

THE BIG PICTURE. Dr. Parker has for several years been going into Rockwell factories and accomplishing just such a transformation.

That kind of organizational redesign, Mr. Murphy emphasizes, is a key piece of a larger transformation: a "total think-through of how we manage, how we are going to design and posture ourselves to compete long term in world markets."

It starts, Mr. Murphy says, with business strategy. "We have 54 different businesses. We've got to understand where those businesses are going, what are the opportunities, what markets are we going to stay in, which ones are we not, how are we going to get where we want to go, what are the key issues of that."

Then, he says, the rethinking—and in many cases, the redesigning—must focus on six major considerations:

- Organizational structure and the management process.
- Manager skills and capabilities.
- Management style.
- Manager succession.
- Reward systems.
- Technology.

And it's crucial, he adds, that "when you change any one of those, you have to go back and look at how the others are impacted. You don't want to treat any one in isolation."

SOMETHING OF VALUE. Rockwell has a conviction about what kind of "future organization" it's going to take to compete: It will be an organization that has pivoted to a whole new orientation.

"We are evolving a value system," Mr. Murphy points out, "that is putting emphasis on certain things we think it's going to take to be a winner. No. 1 is teamwork. No. 2 is teamwork. No. 3 is teamwork.

"We want to evolve a strong value system that applies to everyone, not just managers. It happens over time. But we have defined it. And it is being articulated by top management. We are beginning to weave it into the fabric of how we manage the company, deep into the organization."

But to make all of this mean anything, he emphasizes, there must be a profound change in managerial style within a whole new and "non-repressive" organization.

A change to what?

"The distinguishing feature of these [new] organizations is that high commitment by employees is presumed in the basic design of the organization," Dr. Parker says. "The organization is designed to *generate* high commitment, to fully *utilize* high commitment for gains [business and human] and to *depend* upon high commitment for its effectiveness."

The traditional organization, he notes, has been around a long time, and because it worked, it was adopted by successive waves of managers. It forces workers to comply with stated goals. It can operate with low commitment because of an elaborate set of rules, regulations, policies, and practices that are designed to produce reliable performance and worker compliance. Labor is managed as a variable cost in that system; employees are viewed as expendable spare parts. Reaction to problems is piecemeal. Reaction to change, to the demands of customers, is slow and ineffective. The organization is seen as a machine, running on rules and regulations and not as a total system with interrelated parts.

"That organization is designed for top production efficiency and management control," Dr. Parker analyzes. "In today's dynamic competitive business environment that's not enough."

The new competitive climate alone, he believes, puts the "just-adequate" approach at risk. But worker expectations have also changed and the traditional approach, Dr. Parker finds, is beginning to break down also "because it too severely violates current expectations."

Aside from high commitment and teamwork, Mr. Murphy says, there are other "hallmarks" of the new management style Rockwell is evolving: A focus on value-added to the customer, an entrepreneurial spirit, a willingness to take personal "ownership" of and responsibility for the business, and to take "prudent" risks. Managers scrutinize their policies on the basis of these questions: Are they needed, do they really make a difference, do they add value to the business? Corporate staff roles are being reshaped into "leadership roles that add value and are not just in the business of being administrative focal points.

"You won't see a heavy demarcation between functional staffs, where they think they are entities unto themselves. They are coming to understand the totality of the business and the need to operate as an integrated management system," Mr. Murphy says.

Then there's the vital need, he contends, to "leverage" the link between people and technology. Installing new technology to be competitive is not enough.

Dr. Parker explains:

" [Technology] helps solve the problem over here, on management's side, but creates hell over there, on the worker's side. Companies tend not to worry about the fallout, the layoffs. New technology actually is driving a change in plant organizations. The winners will be those

Dr. Warrington S. Parker Jr., 47, a rock-hard 225-pounder, once dreamed of professional sports as a career. He did coach and teach at a school in Detroit, worked on a Ford Motor assembly line, and kept books and carried a lot of mortar for his father's construction business. He was an assistant professor at the University of Michigan before joining Rockwell in 1978 where he's now director-organization and executive development.

...who recognize the need for a complementary state-of-the-art social structure."

Dr. Parker has shepherded five new plants and one existing one through a design process to create that new "social structure."

The design process Rockwell is instituting in its plants allows managers who are starting new organizations to question everything that was done in the past. That way, they can create a more competitive organization and enable existing plants to redesign in the same way.

What Rockwell does, Dr. Parker says, is what most organizations don't know how to do: give managers a method for making choices that result in an effective organization.

The process begins with a design team—the plant manager, people reporting to him, and a cross section of all others—from the shop floor to secretaries. Topics up for discussion include business objectives of the organization—such as return on investment or inventory levels—the technological purpose (what it's trying to produce and the technology needed), the flow of work from raw material to product, and an organizational structure that will meet business goals and whatever is needed to get a highly committed workforce. Worker wants most likely will be: Challenging work, respect, involvement, adequate reward, open communications, and trust in the organization.

DECISIONS

The team will decide what the organization stands for, what its credo is. Perhaps it's lowest cost and highest quality. The team will consider who will be making demands on the organization—externally (the division, corporate executives, the government, OSHA, the local community) or internally—and how to respond. It will identify all of the tasks involved in reaching goals, how the plant should be laid out, and what the organizational structure should be: teams, or teams within groups, and whether they should be formed around technology or in natural work groups.

"When it comes to deciding how many people there should be in this or that group or team," Dr. Parker says, "we pretend that everyone can do everything—maintenance, machine operation, hiring, firing, pay, customer service. Then you decide what they can't do and kick them out. These become support people."

The designers consider the reward system, whether it will be all salaried, skill-based pay, or something else. They decide how teams should operate, whether members should rotate and learn all skills, whether team members should evaluate who's ready to move on, whether the team has the final say on new hires entering its circle. And the design team can, and generally does, opt for an egalitarian "culture," with status symbols eliminated.

"They end up with what they want to end up with," Dr. Parker says. "You cannot decree these things. Everything is a consensus. We will not leave a design until there's a consensus. The only one with the authority to say, 'I can't go along with that' is the plant manager."

What you end up with in terms of a leaner organization is a minimum of worker job classes, a minimum of management layers, and fewer managers—who now are more "facilitators" than they are managers.

THE UNCONVINCED. It's difficult, Dr. Parker cautions, to bring such changes to an existing plant in the face of years of tradition.

"Older workers might say, 'Just leave me on my machines. I don't want any new skills.' There's an element of self-preservation—'If I'm the only one who knows how to do this, I'm O.K.' And not everyone can survive under the new system," Dr. Parker says.

Of the overall corporate scene, Mr. Murphy adds: "Some managers are moving faster than we ever dreamed. Others still don't understand what's happening. We are trying not to jam this down any throats, but they have got to understand—by listening to Mr. Anderson and Mr. Beall, through training programs, by seeing that managers who are good radiators of this style of management are moving into key positions."

Rockwell has put a lot of emphasis on succession and depth of management to "preserve continuity, a sense of history, a perspective on a particular business," Mr. Murphy says.

"We got caught up, like a lot of companies, in the practice of moving whiz kids, bright M.B.A.s, into positions before they really knew the business. We also got ourselves in the trap of moving people too quickly—to where we almost developed a culture where a bright young manager, if he wasn't moved every two years, felt there was something wrong with him. We've changed that. We've said we expect people to stay in jobs long enough to really know their business, to be measured on how well they've done. The key is having people behind them who also are very knowledgeable and can step right in," he says.

The total "think-through" of how Rockwell should manage had to include something else: a reward system. Explains Mr. Murphy: "To be consistent with our desire to put more responsibility with the business unit, we're designing our reward system to focus not so much on performance of the corporation—although that's a part of it—but on the performance of those individual businesses. And we're designing these reward systems to emphasize and reward teamwork as well as individual contributions."

One business segment, for example, has an incentive system whereby employees are rewarded only on the basis of the business' performance. "And has that had an impact!" Mr. Murphy says with a grin.

Merit pay and bonuses are still around. And so, Mr. Murphy points out, are the best of the traditions and corporate culture of Rockwell units such as the former Collins Radio Co., and Allen-Bradley Co.

"We want to build on the best of what they have," he says, "and link it to the kind of overall culture we're developing. Do we want every business to go in lock step? Absolutely not. We are not trying to put a straitjacket on Rockwell."

But there is one goal that Dr. Parker sees eventually engaging everyone at Rockwell: "We have not yet tapped all the things that excite people to work." ∎

Robert H. Murphy, 48, is a native of Long Beach, Calif., and a dedicated sailboater. But Rockwell's 54 business units see him far more often than his 36-footer sees him. Now vice president-management and organization, he was vice president of organization and management resources in 1980 when the corporation began its redesign into an "organization of the future," a process he oversees.

The next discussion will focus on another Rockwell organization where the design process was initiated without maintaining its integrity, a mistake I ensured not to repeat.

CHAPTER XX
AN ACCOUNT OF A FAILURE — ROCKWELL SCIENCE CENTER, THOUSAND OAKS, CA, SOCIO-TECHNICAL SYSTEMS DESIGN PROCESS

This account explores a failed attempt to implement the Socio-Technical Systems Design Process while designing the organization to transfer a product from research to manufacturing. The product in question was Gallium Arsenide, a dark-gray crystalline compound crucial in manufacturing microelectronic components such as solar cells and semiconductors. The transfer was from Rockwell's Science Center in Thousand Oaks, CA, to a dedicated new manufacturing facility.

The success of the design process hinges on the involvement of the highest-ranking General Manager, who must present the business's immutable goals, known as the "Business Givens" (the 3-5 immutable business goals that the design must achieve). However, in this case, the General Manager was preoccupied and delegated the task to the Chief Engineer of the Gallium Arsenide project. The Chief Engineer's "Givens" included a controversial goal: owning the manufacturing process rather than Rockwell. When the General Manager learned of this objective, Rockwell initiated legal action against the Chief Engineer and ultimately won the case. I was deposed as part of the lawsuit.

Dr. Calvin H. P. Pava from Harvard Business School assisted me in the design process. He recognized the potential ethical dilemma posed by advanced technology, which could either benefit humanity or be used to manipulate people. This perspective is discussed in *The Palgrave Handbook of Organizational Change Thinkers* by Douglas Austrom and C. Ordowich (2019). I never allowed this mistake to happen again in my change work at Rockwell.

He assisted me in the design process. He recognized the potential ethical dilemma posed by advanced technology, which could either benefit humanity or be used to manipulate people. This perspective is discussed in *The Palgrave Handbook of Organizational Change Thinkers* by Douglas Austrom and C. Ordowich (2019). I never allowed this mistake again in my change work at Rockwell. See the account-- A Business Turnaround next.

———————————

CHAPTER XXI
ACCOUNT OF THE ROCKWELL SEMI-CONDUCTORS DIVISION. NEWPORT BEACH. CA

Implemented the McKinsey 7' S Model A Business Turnaround

The 7's change model was implemented as a total system, strategically driven analysis and design process. The President, general managers, direct reports, and a multi-disciplinary, multi-division level team completed the process. The size of the team ranged from 30-40 members. The change process started with a two-day workshop. I initiated the change process and advised Richard Fellow and Dr. Robert Miles, who guided the design team through the process. Dr. Miles, who had experience in the semiconductor business, was influenced by this process and later wrote two books about how he expanded the change process I started at the Semiconductor business. Bob followed the President of Semiconductors to Apple and another company, expanding what I began at Semiconductors.

As described previously, the 7's "fit" concept is fundamental to modern organizational design. It emphasizes aligning the design of an organization with its strategy and other contingency factors. A well-designed organization that fits its strategy achieves better financial performance, while misfits lead to disorganization and reduced performance (Schlevogt, 2002). The better the fit of an organization's key components, the better the business performance and employee well-being.

During the work with the Semiconductor Division in Newport, CA, a two-day workshop was held with the key goal of assisting the team in going through an analysis process using the systems framework we developed to gain clarity about their competitive business environment, vision, and business strategy, and how the organization was structured to execute the strategy. Once there was agreement on the business strategy, the team completed the analysis of the current organization structure, processes, systems, people skills, and capabilities to determine their ability to implement the strategy successfully. Oftentimes, there was no agreement on the business strategy, requiring rework. This usually required several meetings to gain agreement.

Divisional Level Redesign Process

The total system approach to division-level redesign critically depends on a robust process of analysis, learning, and change. This process started differently from the organizational planning and design process used in the redesign of the core strategic processes in the plants or businesses. At the time we started implementing this part of the large-scale organizational change strategy, the division leaders were not aware that a response to their organizational problems could be the redesign of their division core processes. This division analysis process was developed to gain this awareness.

Executive Workshop

The single most powerful element of the process architecture for facilitating the work of division analysis and redesign among leaders at the top is a series of carefully designed and facilitated monthly-to-quarterly executive workshops devoted to the transformation effort. These workshops were designed and led by the division's general manager with adequate process consulting support. They needed to be regularly scheduled as part of the division calendar.

Bi-monthly workshops lasting two or three days seemed to best fit the rhythm of the division redesign process. Having these events in an informal off-site location did more than minimize interruptions. It also removed the executives and team members from their normal routines and symbols of position and status, enabling them to shift into a division-level perspective rather than their usual business or functional point of view.

Having a multiple-layer team helped shorten the cycle of learning and opened lines of communication to those in charge of all parts of the enterprise. Managers with firsthand knowledge of the basic businesses and functions became directly involved in the process of dialogue and decision-making about the changes needed. Involving third-tier managers and below in the leadership forum added energy to the transformation effort because these managers often were the ones looking for signals about how to be successful over the next five to ten years and were, therefore, very interested in the new performance agenda.

An expanded team also helped to speed the initial process of executive alignment with the redesign process by avoiding the problem of selective filtering of information down through the first three layers.

The bi-monthly or quarterly series of executive workshops also served as a primary vehicle for developing, orchestrating, and refining the design process. The executive workshops helped sustain focus on these initiatives and exposed leaders to new concepts, frameworks, best practices, and benchmark data to maintain the process of quantum improvement. Participants in the workshops brought their in-depth knowledge of how their part of the organization worked. They were asked to adopt the perspective of the organization during all or most of the workshop agenda.

The systems framework for leading division-level redesign outlined earlier became operational in these executive workshops. Each workshop's agenda combined redesign planning and follow-through with just-in-time education and problem-solving around obstacles encountered. New transformation concepts and ideas were introduced, discussed, and vetted before being introduced into the mainstream of change initiatives that made up the overall transformation effort. Other ideas and programs that had outlived their purpose or did not align with the transformation agenda were weeded out.

Executive education and involvement at the beginning and throughout a divisional transformation had a similar effect. It opened executives' minds to new ideas and sensitized them in a very personal way to the intellectual and emotional hurdles that others would have to clear if the division transformation was to be successful.

Lastly, it was essential to have timely communication with the organization community about the progress of the executive workshops. If this was not done, informal grapevines would fill the gaps. In division transformation, communication could not wait until all the pieces had come together. The organization at large needed to develop its understanding of the process and its requirements as they became clearer to the executive leadership group during the division analysis and redesign journey.

Cascades

Education and involvement opportunities created by the division team needed to cascade down through the organization as soon as the basic nature of the division change had taken shape. When education and involvement were aligned with the division change agenda and implemented throughout the organization in a timely manner, tailored to fit the audience at each level and in every part of the enterprise, the effect was one of greatly leveraging the influence of the Division General Manager as a transformational leader.

Business Results

Rockwell's Semiconductor Products Division (SPD) completed this approach and achieved a positive turnaround in results. These results were achieved without implementing the organizational planning and design process to redesign the core processes. The division gained greater clarity about its strategy, got the functions to work together better, and focused by eliminating product development that was not part of the core business. The semiconductor business situation, change process, and results were discussed.

In 1986, the Semiconductor Products Division of Rockwell Corporation's Electronics Operations achieved a profit for the first time since 1980—$12 million, which was $5 million above plan. In 1987, the division made a $34 million profit, which represented a $54 million improvement since 1984 when the division suffered a $20 million loss. This remarkable turnaround began in 1983.

The Situation in 1983

In 1983, the division—then known as the Electronic Devices Division (EDD)—had two product lines: semiconductor products (calculators, semiconductor circuits, and circuits for the electronic games market) and telecommunications products (circuits and modems). At that time, approximately half of the division's business was tied to the electronic games market, an area that was experiencing a severe downturn.

EDD was hit hard by order cancellations and returns. As a result, the division had massive inventories and a low backlog, and it faced the prospect of significant layoffs. At the same time, the growing telecommunications product area, which accounted for about 48 percent of division sales and its only profits, was suffering from inadequate management attention and limited resources.

The telecommunications business was viewed as a second priority in a division that had traditionally been closely tied to the semiconductor industry. Of the 15 division executives on the division's incentive compensation plan, only one was in the telecommunications business.

There was a notable lack of strategic focus within the division, and its charter was constantly changing. This situation was exacerbated by the division having experienced considerable turnover in top management. During the previous four years, there had been two essentially nonresident EDD presidents.

Separate marketing, engineering, and manufacturing organizations supported each of the division's two product lines, a situation that resulted in redundant activities, battles for resources, and constant friction. An inflexible and cumbersome contract approval process also impacted the division's ability to function effectively.

The lack of strong division-wide management had encouraged the emergence of several product and functional empires paralleling the division organization, and product area managers were quick to establish what they saw as appropriate priorities for their individual departments. The long-term health of the total organization had virtually been neglected, and division resources were constantly being pulled in all directions.

There was little communication among various departments in the division. A provincial type of culture had developed in which people jockeyed for survival and scrambled to avoid the blame for anything bad that happened. People tied their own security and success to that of their product line manager. The result was a win/lose attitude where the members of a product organization purposely kept information from others outside that group. Any change was viewed as a potential threat. The emphasis was on individual survival. Moreover, people would not admit to or even talk about problems. There was a division-wide tendency to tell senior managers what they wanted to hear.

The net result was a short-term orientation. Little consideration was given to the long-term health of the entire organization, a situation that was reinforced by a bonus system that rewarded individual performance regardless of total division performance. The incentive system was overwhelmingly weighted in favor of the overall performance of Rockwell International. The division could lose money, and incentive compensation program (ICP) recipients at SPD would still earn a bonus if Rockwell did well overall.

The division was clearly in need of a turnaround, one that would require a multidisciplinary effort that would culminate in a new strategic focus building on division strengths and acknowledging market trends, several structural and systems changes to facilitate the accomplishment of new business goals, and a fundamentally different organizational culture and management style.

A Fresh Approach

A major step toward the turnaround occurred in 1983 with the appointment of a new president of the division. The President had spent the 12 previous years at Fairchild Camera & Instrument Company. Under his leadership, and with the support of group leadership at the level of Rockwell's Dallas-based Electronics Operations (EO), including the Electronics Operations President, the division began to address its problems.

Creating A New Climate: The Chartreuse Strategy

During his conversations with people, the president discovered that the basic talent was available in the division but that it just wasn't being used. Division leadership, direction, interdepartmental communications, and teamwork were missing.

It was clear that the mindset of the organization had to be changed. The President later reflected: "I was willing to try anything. It didn't matter if I had to paint the building chartreuse to change the pervasive attitude of doom and gloom and business as usual, and I constantly told people so." Somehow, that quote was made into a sort of an inside joke around here, and the actions that I later took became known as "the chartreuse strategy."

One of the first significant actions taken was to rename the division the Semiconductor Products Division (SPD). This action was seen as a way of making people realize that the old EDD way of thinking—short-term thinking, the "us versus them" attitudes between functions and the two businesses within the division—was a thing of the past and that everything done from then on would be fundamentally different

Overview of Organizational Changes

During this early period, when performance was extremely poor, the President made several organizational changes to address some of the key problems in the division. These isolated efforts to bring about organizational improvement were later expanded on and integrated into a division-wide "organizational excellence change process," which, under the President's direction, helped the business define and systematically execute its turnaround strategy (discussed in more detail later in the case).

Human Resources

The President believed that increasing emphasis on the human resources function would elevate people's issues to a position of primacy within the organization and, thus, positively impact the SPD culture. He recognized that he needed a vehicle for making the required organizational and attitudinal changes, and he saw Human Resources as the natural framework within which to execute the initial changes.

A key objective was to reinforce the idea throughout SPD that the issues on the employees' minds were vital to the organization's success, and concern for these issues needed to be communicated. Giving the function added credibility helped to improve the communication process. Moreover, it was clear to the President that some management changes would be necessary, and the Human Resources function under the leadership of the director would be an invaluable asset in the drive to bring in new, highly qualified, and motivated people.

The Organizational Study

One of the first activities carried out by the new Human Resources function was an organizational study. An external consultant assisted the director in carrying out the study.

The study yielded several conclusions about the situation within the division. SPD was not structured to support its business. The division did not have sufficient talent to meet the technical/market challenges. There was a lack of teamwork among the executive staff and elsewhere throughout the organization. Communications were nonexistent throughout the division from top to bottom and between the two major product groups (semiconductors and telecommunications).

Management had limited credibility because of the frequent turnover of presidents and the resultant frenetic shifts in strategies, policies, and priorities. Finally, the organization had become totally demoralized by the years of instability and severe layoffs.

The President's immediate reactions to the study conclusions were (1) to aggressively recruit talent, beginning with the executive staff, and (2) to begin to develop an effective communication program. Another objective was to change the attitude and improve the teamwork among the Level II and III managers in SPD.

At the core of these changes was a consolidation of both businesses into one functional management team reporting directly to the division president. The team included the heads of Engineering, Production Operations, Operations Support, Major Programs, and Marketing. A new division staff was also set up, consisting of human resources, finance, and planning heads. Later, in 1985, an executive vice president and a director of strategic planning were hired. In addition, Quality was subsequently elevated to a direct report position, and Far Eastern Operations and European Operations were established as direct reports.

Marketing and Sales

As a first step in building a new executive team, the marketing function was streamlined to improve its effectiveness. The marketing organizations of SPD's former semiconductor and telecommunications product groups were consolidated and placed under a vice president of marketing who reported directly to the President. This new structure eliminated much of the organizational duplication that had previously existed. Further, it established the foundation for evolving a global market orientation consisting of Domestic Sales, Far Eastern Operations, and European Operations.

In addition, steps were taken to staff Marketing with personnel who possessed a range of functional and technical expertise. Some experienced non-division people familiar with the telecommunications market were brought into the organization. Other employees who were recognized for their solid overall technical marketing performance were hired. The purpose of these moves was to foster an increasingly professional approach to the marketing function, to support new business directions, and to instill a more sophisticated and systematic marketing philosophy in the division.

Engineering

The President then turned his attention to establishing a new sense of pride, focus, and accountability in engineering. Prior to his arrival, the Engineering staff felt that they had been treated like second-class citizens. When slowdowns in orders occurred, it was often Engineering that suffered the first and most severe layoffs. A lot of resources were spread over many different products, but not much R&D was done in any one product or area. Only a relatively small number of products under development were ever successfully brought to market.

An individual was promoted to direct a consolidated engineering function for the division. The director helped Engineering become a highly focused, disciplined, and time-sequenced function for new product development. The initial product design process dramatically improved due to increased process discipline, improved front-end planning, workstations, computer networking, new CAD tools, CAM/CIM interfaces, and fast-turn prototypes. Under the director, the average product design cycle, which took 36 months in 1984, was reduced to 18 months by 1987.

The director also created a people-motivated environment. Formal project teams were initiated, and instant compensation was utilized to publicly reward the performance of engineering teams that completed their projects on time or ahead of schedule. Increased recognition of engineering accomplishments was also reinforced through activities such as pizza parties with the director of engineering for successful project contributions.

As a result of his interventions, the amount of time required from design conception to manufacturing significantly decreased. Simultaneously, the number of new products introduced to the marketplace dramatically increased.

Production Operations

The President also replaced SPD's production operations director with a new hire who had built a good reputation at Texas Instruments. However, shortly after the new director took over, he made drastic changes in production methods and personnel that sent morale plummeting. He was not a team player, and he never left his office to mix with his people. A little more than a year after the new production operations director was hired, he was removed, and a new director was promoted from within the organization. He had developed a superb reputation within the division for his varied production experiences and his ability to lead people.

The director introduced a highly disciplined, quality-focused, cost-sensitive manufacturing process. Extreme attention to detail, including cleanliness of facilities and analysis of every single defect, were significant contributors to improved product yield. The director's introduction of manufacturing systems, such as PROMIS—a production control tracking mechanism—and other process control vehicles, such as statistical quality control, were also instrumental in achieving product yield improvements.

In addition, the director introduced a strong team-oriented approach to decision-making throughout production operations, including the use of quality circles (discussed in more detail later in this case). Multidisciplinary production operations project teams were formed that included employees from other SPD functions when appropriate. The teams were tasked to assist with yield improvements, product defect analysis, and other productivity enhancement programs. Instant compensation was publicly used to recognize team achievements in such areas as reduced product cycle time and increased product yield. Operator recognition programs were also initiated, along with the use of pizza parties to recognize significant departmental contributions.

Cooperative teamwork established between Production Operations and Engineering also emerged as a critical ingredient in the improved success achieved by both functions. For example, the time-to-market strategic initiative was greatly accelerated due to the introduction of cross-functional project task teams and the establishment of a Project Review Board.

Changes in staffing practices at all manufacturing facilities also contributed to production improvements. Rigid hiring standards were enforced: engineers hired into the function were required to have college degrees. Experienced engineers from within SPD emerged to run the division's three manufacturing operations.

In the years following such actions, the improvements in product yields, quality, and costs at SPD's El Paso, Mexicali, and Newport Beach operations were dramatic. For example, the measure of equivalent finished goods for one of SPD's products—the number of final good products that were eventually shipped per final wafer start—climbed from a low of 2 in mid-1984 to 54 by mid-1987. In devices, the measure of assembled leads per operator per day rose from 14,000 in 1983 to an average of 25,000 in 1986. The average throughput time for the division's products fell from 117 days in 1982 to 38 days in 1986. Gross inventory also decreased from $52 million in early 1985 to $24 million by 1987—even though the division increased sales from $162 million in 1985 to $202 million by 1987.

Quality

In 1985, Quality was also established as a separate function, with a director reporting directly to the President. According to the director, the division's new emphasis on quality (a strategic thrust) and the introduction of customer action teams were important factors associated with the dramatic improvement in the level of quality achieved with SPD products during the first two years after the President arrived. A reduction in the return rate from 5.1 percent to 0.2 percent from Far East customers provided much impetus in helping SPD capture 85 percent of the FAX modem market in Japan and 63 percent of the worldwide market in 1986.

A customer action team consisted of key SPD personnel representing Design Engineering, Product Engineering, Manufacturing Field Applications, and Quality, together with some of their counterparts in the customer organization. Each team attempted to identify the causes of quality problems and to develop corrective action plans. In many instances, the causes of quality problems on one product line were found to affect other product lines. Thus, the output of these teams had a snowballing effect on product quality throughout SPD.

Major Programs

A Major Programs function was also established, with the appointment of a vice president who reported directly to the president. This was an important step as it provided a focused interface between the division and major customers. The function hired highly credible, experienced division people with diversified backgrounds to serve as program managers and to work in cooperation with the other functions. Neither the Major Programs Office nor its program managers were given formal or sign-off authority. Instead, the division's functional heads retained all the authority. Yet, due to the integrated teamwork that had been established in the division, the Major Programs Office, under the vice president's leadership, had evolved to become a strong catalyst in pulling the functional areas together to meet customer needs and requirements.

Finance

An individual who had been manager of the division's silicon-producing facility was promoted to controller, a change that brought new dimensions in terms of functional focus and inter-functional cooperation to Finance. As a result, the financial function provided integrated, multifunctional coordination in helping the division address two specific strategic thrusts: the establishment of a management tracking and control system and improvement of gross profit levels and asset management. For example, SPD asset management improved dramatically. Assets decreased from $109 million in 1985 to $72 million in 1986 and to $70 million in 1987, despite significantly increased sales and profits.

Inter-functional Cooperation

Much work was done within the organization to improve multifunctional integration. An Inventory Council, which is made up of financial managers, production control managers, and marketing product line managers, was implemented to put more emphasis on reducing inventory levels. A divisional Capital Committee was established to keep purchase levels down. Both committees were tangible responses to specific strategic thrusts that had been targeted for action by the SPD president and members of SPD's key manager group.

Opening Communications

To open communications within the division, meetings at different levels of the organization were initiated.

Results Meetings

The president began to hold daily results meetings in which he and his direct reports would discuss the problems that had developed over the previous 24 hours and then devise an action plan for their resolution. The next day, the appropriate level II manager would spend five minutes reporting on whether the previous day's suggestion had worked. The entire group would then develop a suggested course of correction if necessary.

The group would move on to discuss problems confronting level II managers in other functional areas. This process helped to build a sense of cooperation and urgency at SPD because the corrective actions were decided largely by consensus, and the frequency of the meetings prohibited slippage in execution. As many of the recurring division problems began to dissipate, the results meetings were cut back to twice a week.

Staff Meetings

A series of monthly staff meetings was initiated in which the president and his direct reports would provide input on their overall concerns about the division. The purpose of the meetings was to find out what was on the minds of the direct reports. The president openly solicited agenda items for the meetings to give his people the chance to blow off some steam.

Business Review Meetings

Monthly business review meetings also included the President and his direct reports. The focus of these meetings was to present state-of-the-business information on SPD, the semiconductor industry, and Rockwell International as a whole. The overriding intent of the business review meetings was to broaden the thinking of the direct reports and to heighten their awareness of how SPD's performance related to the corporation and the industry.

Department Meetings

Department meetings were held on a quarterly basis and included the division president, the level II manager responsible for a given department, and the level III managers responsible for corporate functions. At these meetings, the level III managers made presentations, reviewing their functional areas for the preceding quarter. The focus of the department meetings was to bring the third layer of management into the review process and to give these managers additional exposure in the overall running of the division.

Employee Meetings

To enhance communications between the three management levels and production employees, the President held semiannual meetings that included all the employees of the division. During the first hour, he would make overall announcements on product development or production-level milestones, employee promotions, and so forth. He would also provide a summary of industry and corporate developments that were influencing the division, how the division had performed in relation to production targets during the previous six months, and the next set of targets for the ensuing year.

The second part of the meeting was devoted to a question-and-answer period in which the President would address both prepared and spontaneous inquiries on the whole range of employee concerns.

"Coffee Klatches"

The President also promoted meetings of several (five to seven) employees in an informal session either with him or with a level II or level III manager. These meetings became popularly known as "Coffee Klatches" and were understood to be completely confidential in nature. The intent was to provide an informal channel of communication regarding employee concerns. Bargaining unit employees were chosen at random, and the attending manager was encouraged to promptly address the issues raised.

"Lunch With the President"

As an extension of the department meetings, the President started a practice that became known as the "lunch with the President" series. Approximately twice a month, he would invite a level III manager to meet informally with him to discuss department and individual issues that were of current interest to the managers.

A Test of the Communication Process

Just as the organizational changes were being implemented, Atari, one of the division's principal customers in the electronic games market, canceled all its orders. The elimination of these orders cut SPD's backlog in half, and the division suddenly faced a financial crisis. The entire workforce was immediately put on a four-day week, and the President ordered massive layoffs.

According to the business manager of the labor union that represented the division's bargaining unit, "It's a good thing that the President had done all the work communicating with these people that he did before that happened because otherwise, all hell would have broken out over the layoffs. As it happened, the level II and III managers who were responsible for the functional areas sat down with our people and explained the situation. We didn't like it any better, but at least we understood why the layoffs were happening, and we appreciated having it explained to us."

A More Fundamental Approach to Change

The President of Rockwell's Electronics Operations (EO) provided staff support to assist in the SPD turnaround effort. When it was determined in SPD's internal organizational study that significant improvements would probably be needed in such difficult-to-change areas as strategy consensus, organizational teamwork between functions to execute strategy, and management style, the President of Rockwell's Electronics Operations and the Operations Vice President of Human Resources asked the Electronics Operations director of management and organizational resources to visit the division to conduct an organizational diagnosis of the strengths and weaknesses of the business, to assess the validity of perceived needs, and to assist as appropriate. The resulting diagnosis validated the organizational concerns and needs.

In examining the findings and associated implications, the director of organization and human resources worked closely with the director of Human Resources, myself, and two senior Electronics Operations staff officers. We concluded that the organizational changes that had already been implemented (that is, reducing staff, reviewing products, and conducting employee meetings) would not be sufficient to make the business viable. Fundamental issues, such as what business SPD should be in, were yet to be addressed and resolved.

Thus, the director of organization and human resources, after the planning design we conducted, recommended that SPD implement a comprehensive division-wide organizational change process to assist with and accelerate division progress on a systematic basis. The process has since become known in Rockwell International as "organizational excellence," which consists of two large-scale organizational change strategies. The next step was to discuss the plan with the President of Semiconductors.

During the presentation to the President, recommendations, including the use of off-site workshops with high-talent executives from all division disciplines and locations, were discussed. In addition, the presentation focused on how this process would help participants see the division as a total system, assess division issues, identify needed changes, and establish shared ownership and teamwork in bringing about desired division improvements.

At the conclusion of the presentation, the President stated that he had been looking for a systematic approach to collectively address division-wide issues. He went on to say that he supports the organizational excellence philosophy and agreed to use the process with a few modifications. The President then asked the director of organization resources to serve as the advisor and change facilitator for the organizational change process.

The decision was made to wait approximately four to six months before implementation so that some ongoing changes could be completed. The President also committed to hiring a full-time division person who could work with the director of organization and human resources and the director of semiconductors HR director to manage the process.

In the meantime, to expand employee involvement in the change effort, a Division Advisory Council was formed to examine productivity-oriented issues and to create new programs as necessary. The council included two directors, a newly appointed manager of productivity, and two senior EO staff managers.

Employee Circles

Commonly referred to as Quality Circles, employee circles were one of the newly created programs. It was believed that if properly implemented, employee circles would provide a focal point for the division to begin participative management techniques and teamwork, would illustrate that employees desired to contribute to the success of their organization, and would demonstrate that management and union officials could work together cooperatively for the good of the business. It was decided from the beginning that the union would be an active partner in the establishment of employee circles at SPD. The human resources director, industrial relations manager, and director of organization and human resources approached the union business manager and her chief steward for input and participation.

The first step in the establishment of employee circles at SPD was the formation of a Circle to provide guidance to ensure circle success and to find necessary resources. The human resources manager provided professional support in the form of a circle facilitator. Within the context of this overall environment, the employee circle flourished.

The President's Role in the Leadership Development Programs

The President of the business was the instructor for this account in The Rockwell Executive Leadership Development Programs. He discussed his role and answered the program participants' questions. This organizational change was an example of what can be done, leading to a business turnaround, from losing profits to making a profit. The discussion of the Semiconductor's case focused on organizational change in the programs. The participants in the leadership programs were active in discussions about the account and were impressed with the leadership of the business.

Review Dr Miles expansion of this approach he expanded to large-scale organizational change in his *Corporate Transformation*.

Next, additional Accounts of Rockwell businesses completed the Socio-Technical Systems design process with positive business results.

CHAPTER XXII
ADDITIONAL ACCOUNTS OF BUSINESS RESULTS

1. **Rockwell's Tactical Systems Division**
   - ○ Located in Duluth, GA, this defense business continuously improved its systems and processes through a customer-driven, team-based organization. Key achievements include:
     - **Market Share:** Competitively won 100% of the market share from their competitor, Martin Marietta.
     - **Labor Efficiency:** Reduced work labor hours by 40% while increasing volume.
     - **Operational Success:** Achieved two years of continuous operation without a missile failure.

2. **North American Aircraft (NAA) – Tulsa Division**
   - ○ This large aerostructures division, located in Tulsa, OK, implemented a redesign with a rank-and-file members, union, and management design team. Key outcomes include:
     - **Supplier Recognition:** Named Boeing's Number One aerostructures supplier worldwide, primarily due to responsiveness to customer needs.
     - **Competitive Advantage:** Improved competitive position, winning profitable contracts for two new 777 programs.
     - **Quality Assurance:** Products now bypass Boeing's receiving inspection process, indicating high quality.
     - **Inventory Management:** Reduced inventory levels by 20%, enhancing return-on-assets.

3. **Rockwell Automotive Truck Transmissions Plant, Laurinburg, NC**
   - ○ A start-up business targeting well-established competitors, this plant focused on customer-centric, self-managed teams. Key indicators of success include:
     - **Market Penetration:** Captured approximately 15% of the heavy truck transmission market (North American Class 8) in less than three years.

- **Efficiency Gains:** Achieved a 41% reduction in manufacturing hours per transmission (from 1990 to 1991).
- **Scrap Reduction:** Reduced scrap by 25% (from 1991 to 1992).

4. **The Startup of Two New Automotive Manufacturing Plants**
   - With the assistance of Paul Hulbert, an external organizational consultant from Procter & Gamble, a leading company in starting up new plants using this design process, we worked together to implement the organizational design process for two manufacturing plants: the York, South Carolina front axle plant, and the Asheville rear axle plant. These plants experienced the most successful start-ups of new plants that automotive had experienced.
   - The York plant achieved, in 1983, direct labor efficiency of 92% using a 100% standards program, with two job classifications for a 350-person plant, an all-salaried concept, and became a leader in the automotive business for inventory turns. Year to date in 1984, the York plant achieved 18.0 turns versus an automotive average of 5.0 turns. The cost of capital savings associated with improved turns was $80K per year, and the Ford Q1 award was received in 1983.
   - The Asheville facility became profitable six months after start-up. Customer delivery credibility remained over 99% for one year, sales volume was 24.7% above plan, and profit before tax was 9.3 times the plan. The plant had three job classifications, an all-salaried concept, no time clocks, no reserved parking spaces (first come, best spaces), and no separate cafeteria for managers. A goal was to design an egalitarian organization.

5. **Valve Manufacturing Plant**
   - Successfully started up a valve plant in East Kilbride, Scotland.

Each of these design processes focused on optimizing the core business process (the revenue stream), ensuring that the supporting organizations functioned as truly supportive systems. An account of a redesign of a high school implementing a modified Socio-Technical Systems Design Process follows.

CHAPTER XXIII
ACCOUNT OF A SCHOOL REDESIGN. BELLFLOWER HIGH SCHOOL

I implemented the Socio-Technical Systems design process modified for a school

Introduction and Context

I was pleased by Rockwell's request to partner with Bellflower High School (grades 7-12) in Bellflower, CA, to implement a large-scale strategic organizational change strategy that I had previously implemented at Rockwell. I modified the design process specifically for a school setting.

Let's explore this design process, the lessons learned, and the side effects that developed because of the change.

At the time I was introduced to Bellflower High School, I felt it was crucial to update education with job readiness, the ability to compete against smart machines, and the creation of long-term economic value in mind. Education access, equity, and quality must be improved to solve the global education crisis—72 million children of primary education age are not in school (source: www.weforum.org). My interest in education goes back to the values my parents instilled in us regarding the importance of education, and anytime I have the opportunity to work in an educational institution, I take it. Bellflower School is an example of this, which I will discuss next.

I will share the change process I implemented at Bellflower Junior/High School using the Socio-Technical Design process adapted for a school environment. This involved a design team that included union leadership and union members.

The school is in Bellflower, CA. Once considered a suburban town, Bellflower is now an urban city, situated a few miles south of Los Angeles. At the time we began working with the school, it had 130 teachers and staff members serving approximately 2,300 students from various social and economic backgrounds. In 1991, the school's population was extremely diverse, with 35% of the students being white, 36% Hispanic, 18% African American, and 8% Asian. Bellflower High includes both junior high and high school, teaching students in grades seven through twelve.

In 1991, I had the opportunity to apply my knowledge of large-scale organizational design processes at the school. As a result of my work, I learned that the modification of the design process can lead to significant organizational change within a school setting.

The school's Design Process was led by me, supported by Rockwell Corporation, and Barbara Barnes, an Educational Consultant, with assistance from my wife, Brenda A. Parker, MA, Head of a Private Independent School in Los Angeles, CA.

Need for Change

An analysis of Bellflower High School's test scores, the SCANS report, and the national goals for education revealed that students were not being adequately prepared for living and working in the 21st century, where they would need to think critically and acquire the skills and knowledge necessary to be competitive in a global economy. The "SCANS Report" clearly identifies the skills, competencies and personal qualities youth need to compete successfully in the workplace. The commission also charged the U.S. education system with the responsibility of integrating those skills into students' academic preparation, competencies, effective workers can productively us.:

There was sufficient dissatisfaction among Bellflower staff with the instructional strategies, departmentalization, learning opportunities, and the school's design—remnants of the bureaucratic hierarchical, 19th-century industrial model under which much of education still operates—to spark a desire for change.

The Role of the Principal

Recognizing the need for change and the ability to lead that change, the idea that fundamental structural change might be required at Bellflower High School began when the principal attended a National Education Conference on school restructuring in March 1991. This conference focused on changes in the increasingly competitive global environment and the critical role that education must play in the United States for sustained competitiveness.

It was noted that the country had entered a new era, one marked by a highly competitive global economy. In this era, countries will prosper or fail not based on geographical location or the availability of natural resources but on the knowledge of their citizens and their capacity to think, be creative, and continuously learn.

The new reality is that learning is the new form of labor; people work to continuously learn, and knowledge is becoming a key resource for countries. In this context, the conference stressed the need for educational systems to transform themselves to better prepare students for the challenges of the 21st Century.

This experience prompted the principal to reflect on how Bellflower High was currently providing education for its students and to realize that the school's educational system likely needed to change. The seeds for change were planted, and after meeting several months later with Rockwell's Senior Vice President of Human Resources, I became a catalyst in assisting Rockwell to form a partnership with the Bellflower School.

In our meeting, we focused on Rockwell's businesses and how we were implementing large-scale organizational change strategies to remain competitive. We discussed a strategic-driven, large-scale organizational change approach that we were implementing at Rockwell, intending to change all the key elements of the businesses and their interrelationships—business strategy, organization structure, strategic systems and processes that create and deliver customer value, managerial roles and responsibilities, work design, and the reward and promotion systems that lead to high-performance, customer-focused, and team-based organizations. We explored the possible application of this approach to Bellflower High, which needed fundamental change. The principal was interested.

I conducted several exploratory meetings with the principal to determine the readiness and capability of the school to undergo fundamental change, including his leadership ability to lead and support the change, the level of support from the school administrators, the union, teachers, the superintendent, and the school board.

When it became clear that the principal was committed and capable of providing the necessary leadership and that there was enough support within the school and school district, Rockwell agreed to form a partnership. We then proceeded to hire Barbara Barnes, the educational change consultant who had been part of the July meeting and the author of *School Transformation*.

The Design Process

The design process focused on change in all the major elements of the school and the interrelationship between them, including student learning outcomes, values, curriculum, schedule, instructional strategies, instructional technology, grouping of students and teachers, student assessment/evaluation, the structure and role of the administration and "staff" support systems, and parent and community involvement.

Student-Centered, Outcome-Driven Process

We started the process by identifying the student learning outcomes that were important to achieve. These outcomes became one of the key drivers of the transformation design process at Bellflower High. All changes were viewed in the context of achieving these outcomes. They became the overarching organizational goals of the school, with which the faculty could identify and accept. They are like the business "givens," the mandatory organizational goals that start the redesign process in Rockwell's businesses and must be achieved by the new organizational design.

The process began with a collaborative, team-based approach involving teachers, staff, parents, students, and community representatives.

- **Cross-Grade and Cross-Subject Teams:** These teams were formed to develop an integrated curriculum, fostering collaboration among faculty and aligning educational strategies with the desired student outcomes.
- **Involving the School Community:** Unlike in the industry, where specific design teams are formed, the school involved all faculty, students, and parents in the transformation process, ensuring widespread participation and ownership.

It was important for the principal to present the case for fundamental change to the staff, emphasizing the inadequacies of the existing educational system in preparing students for the 21st century.

Key Learnings and Insights

- **Principal's Role:** The principal's active involvement and leadership were crucial for the success of the change process.
- **Dissatisfaction and Vision:** High levels of dissatisfaction with the status quo and a compelling vision for the future were essential to gaining support for the transformation.
- **Student-Centered Focus:** The transformation process was driven by a focus on student learning outcomes, ensuring all changes aligned with these goals.
- **Systematic and Disciplined Process:** A structured systems approach was necessary to manage the change, avoiding fragmented and piecemeal efforts.

Results and Side Effects

The transformation process at Bellflower High School led to several positive outcomes:

1. **Experimentation:** An atmosphere of experimentation allowed for the piloting of new instructional methods and curricula.
2. **Professional Growth:** Teachers demonstrated significant professional growth, taking on greater responsibilities and improving their skills.
3. **Paradigm Shift:** The school experienced a shift from traditional educational models to more collaborative and inclusive approaches.
4. **Improved Communication:** Open lines of communication between faculty, students, and the community were established, enhancing the overall school environment.
5. **Change in Attitudes:** There was a noticeable shift in attitudes among faculty and students, with a greater awareness of the need for modern skills and knowledge. They also learned that industry was helpful in the partnership.

Conclusion

The experience at Bellflower High School highlighted the importance of a well-structured and inclusive change process in educational settings. The collaboration between industry and education provided valuable insights and demonstrated the potential for large-scale organizational change to enhance educational outcomes. *See Appendix C for the Design Phases the school completed.*

CHAPTER XXIV
AN ACCOUNT OF MASTER LABOR UNION–ROCKWELL CONTRACT NEGOTIATIONS CHANGE PROCESS

"Building Trust While Negotiating:" My Experience with the Rockwell Union Management Negotiating Team

I was asked to be a member of the Rockwell Union Management Negotiating team for the Master Union Contracts. I assisted the negotiating team with a process of change called "Building Trust While Negotiating," working alongside John Sivie, a Rockwell internal organization change agent, and Stephen N., a union representative on our team. John and I were trusted by both the company and the labor unions.

The "Building Trust While Negotiating" process intrigued me, and I was eager to become a member of the team. I grew up respecting unions; my dad was a union member. I also worked with unions to pass the Michigan Fair Housing Bill in 1968 and civil rights legislation in Michigan. I had meetings in Detroit at the headquarters of the UAW, Solidarity House on East Jefferson Ave, and attended the memorial for Walter Reuther's brother in Detroit, Michigan. Early in life, I realized that businesses get the union they deserve.

At the time I joined the Corporate Offices, there was a need to improve the relationship. between Rockwell and the unions. Rockwell's management and the labor union leadership agreed to the Master Labor contract negotiations focused on implementing a "win-win," building trust while negotiating change process. The process included negotiating the Master Labor contracts with Rockwell and the UAW in the Aerospace Businesses at Corporate and the Automotive Business, as well as the IBEW contract for the Electronic Businesses.

None of the sixty negotiators could have predicted the results of the negotiations using a non-traditional, issue-oriented, problem-resolution approach.

Outcomes

On June 27, 1990, the negotiation team reached an agreement on the three-year Master Contract in San Diego, California. It was ratified by 85% of the UAW membership present on July 1, 1990. Significant and comprehensive restructuring of the medical insurance program resulted in a cost-containment package, including HMO incentives and a UAW precedent-setting 85-15 indemnity plan.

The parties also reached an agreement on an employee involvement philosophy and involvement in large-scale organizational change through organizational redesign efforts. The union and the company further agreed to establish an independent UAW/Rockwell employee involvement training organization to provide training to enable the union/management and problem-solving approach to continue the job. As a result, Rockwell was now placed in an excellent position to be on the leading edge in its ability to market itself to customers, transform the business through the large-scale change strategy, and improve its ability to increase all the skills of Rockwell employees.

The UAW and Rockwell left the negotiations, stating that they were by far the best negotiations they had participated in with one another. Equally important was that the negotiating team planned to continue this type of issue-oriented, problem-solving approach when they returned to their respective organizations.

A surprising and interesting comment was made by a union member of the negotiating team after the first win-win negotiating success. He said loudly, "If the union believes we won on this issue and management believes it won, we have gotten screwed somewhere."

My participation on the negotiating team was a rewarding experience, seeing the process work. Thanks also go to John Sivie, a Rockwell internal change agent, and Stephanie, a union member who worked with John and me. *See Appendix ??? for more details about the "Win-Win Building Trust While Negotiating" process.*

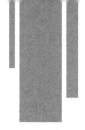

CHAPTER XXV
REFLECTING ON LESSONS LEARNED ABOUT ORGANIZATIONAL CHANGE

- **Leadership is Crucial**
- **Ownership and Vision:** Successful large-scale organizational change must be owned and led by the organization's leader. The leader must articulate a compelling vision and a convincing case for change, mobilizing the organization's members towards a shared future.
- **Leadership Styles:** Effective leaders use a mix of management styles, being directive and participative as needed. They create a sense of urgency and ensure that change is seen as essential for the business's survival and growth.

The Role of the Change Agent is Important

- **Building Trust:** As a change agent, it's crucial to connect personally with executives to build trust and demonstrate confidence in the proposed change strategies.
- **Education and Involvement:** Educating executives about different organizational models and involving them in the change process helps in gaining their support and commitment.

The Importance of Dissatisfaction and Vision

- Change is often driven by dissatisfaction with the status quo or a compelling vision of the future. The more significant the need for change, the more intense the dissatisfaction must be to mobilize action.

Change Agent Skills

- Over time, I developed a set of skills essential for implementing organizational change. These skills were honed through various experiences and applied effectively at Rockwell.
- The design process must consider the socio-psychological needs of employees. This approach enhances employee commitment and performance by aligning organizational goals with employee well-being.

The Importance of a Redesign Team

- A redesign team, including the business leader, direct reports, and a cross-section of employees, is crucial for planning and managing the implementation of change.

Systematic, Disciplined Change Process

- A systematic approach is essential for large-scale organizational change. This process must encompass the entire business and avoid piecemeal changes, which are often ineffective in the long term.

Functional Leaders Working as a Team

- The cooperation of senior functional executives is critical for the success of the business and the motivation of employees.

Communication and Education

- Regular communication about the change process is vital. It ensures that all employees understand the reasons for change and what is required for success.

Time for Change

- Implementing large-scale organizational change takes time. The process involves continuous implementation and adaptation to new demands and expectations.

Involving the People Affected by the Change

- Involving all employees in the change process is crucial. This involvement increases commitment and ownership of the change.

PERSONAL REFLECTIONS

Reflecting on my time as an internal change agent at Rockwell, I believe my effectiveness stemmed from a combination of education, experience, and personal connections with key executives. My academic background, teaching experience, and practical application of organizational theories provided a strong foundation for understanding and implementing change.

I was fortunate to work with knowledgeable individuals who contributed significantly to my understanding and application of change management strategies. The ability to involve and educate executives, align them with the change process, and build trust were crucial components of my success. I learned that the combination of academic training, social skills, and change agent skills helped contribute to my effectiveness at Rockwell. Writing this book has reinforced these lessons.

Reflecting on these experiences has been enlightening. I realize that my decision to leave academia for a corporate position at Rockwell was pivotal in shaping my career. The challenges and successes I encountered have been invaluable learning experiences.

Looking forward, I plan to continue writing about my experiences, including a forthcoming book about my work with my wife at a charter school in Detroit. This next endeavor will explore the application of organizational change principles in an educational setting, continuing my journey of learning and sharing.

EPILOGUE

I wrote this book to discuss my experiences as an internal organizational change agent at Rockwell, where I implemented large-scale strategic change strategies and involved employees in the change process. This includes addressing the socio-psychological needs of employees, which are important for enhancing motivation, commitment, and performance.

As I sit in my study, reflecting on writing this book and what I have learned, I am enjoying a cold beer and looking out at the beautiful, well-kept golf course on the 10th fairway where we live. Our house, nestled among the stunning red rocks of Sedona, AZ, was built with care and love.

I am also reflecting on the joy of life with my beautiful wife of over 61 years, Brenda Ann Cunningham Parker (Gigie), our four accomplished children, and four beautiful, successful grandchildren. Truly a blessing.

APPENDIX A
"BUILDING TRUST WHILE NEGOTIATING" PROCESS
UNION/MANAGEMENT RELATIONS

There was a need to improve relationships between the Unions and Rockwell. The 1980 contract negotiation and subsequent Master Contract negotiations at Rockwell used a non-traditional approach. We implemented a negotiating process to build trust while negotiating. This process will be discussed next.

Introduction

In 1990, Rockwell faced several challenges as negotiators began to prepare for the three-year Aerospace Master Contract labor negotiations with the UAW. The Southern California and Tulsa, Oklahoma labor contracts were up for renewal for 8,000 bargaining unit employees. The settlement at Boeing had set a precedent in aerospace, further supported by Lockheed and McAir's settlements. Other factors facing Rockwell were rising healthcare costs, declining defense budgets, and the opening of a non-union facility in San Bernardino. Based on past negotiating experiences, Rockwell expected the negotiations to be difficult and adversarial. None of the sixty negotiators could have predicted the results of the negotiations using a non-traditional, issue-oriented, problem-resolution approach.

Outcomes

On June 27, 1990, the negotiation team reached an agreement on the three-year Master Contract in San Diego, California. It was ratified by 85% of the UAW membership present on July 1, 1990. Significant and comprehensive restructuring of the medical insurance program resulted in a cost containment package, including HMO incentives and a UAW precedent-setting 85-15 indemnity plan.

The parties also reached an agreement on an employee involvement philosophy and involvement in large-scale organizational change through organizational redesign efforts. The union and the company further agreed to establish an independent UAW/Rockwell employee involvement training organization to provide training to enable the union/management and problem-solving approach to continue the job. As a result, Rockwell was now positioned to be on the leading edge in its ability to market itself to customers, transform the business through the large-scale change strategy, and improve its ability to increase all the skills of Rockwell employees.

The UAW and Rockwell left the negotiations, stating that they were by far the best negotiations they had ever participated in together. Equally important was that the negotiating team planned to continue this type of issue-oriented, problem-solving approach when they returned to their respective organizations. Described below is how the UAW and Rockwell broke out of traditional adversarial roles to form a partnership and relationship based on trust.

The Philosophy/Process

As leadership from the UAW and Rockwell began to closely examine the issues, it became clear that both sides had similar concerns. Both were troubled by increasing healthcare costs and the decline of business in the defense industry. Further, there were several other issues that needed attention, which tended to make the negotiations the most formidable to date. Among these issues were employee involvement and other concerns left unresolved for several years that were carried over from one negotiating session to the next. Added to these mounting and serious issues was the lack of a sound relationship built on mutual trust and respect. The challenge of the negotiations thus became devising a process in which the UAW and Rockwell could work together to satisfy their respective concerns. Problem-solving, built on mutual trust, was a key issue.

Traditionally, building mutual trust was not seen as desirable or important in the negotiation process. Negotiations were seen as a win-lose competition in which each side tried to gain an advantage over the other. This approach to management/labor bargaining, however, has proven to be ineffective, to which most of the participants attested. In most cases, including the settlements cited above, both the union and the company come away from the talks dissatisfied and feeling taken advantage of by the other. Rockwell and the UAW realized that changing this would require a completely new approach to negotiations.

Another impetus to the exploration of different bargaining strategies is the changing environment in which Rockwell and the union exist. As organizations and management practices continue to evolve from traditional to innovative forms, fundamental changes are required to obtain a competitive edge. The shift to fewer hierarchical levels, doing "more with less," achieving flexibility in response to customers, and moving from high control to high performance, high commitment, team-based organizations in which employees are empowered are a few examples of changes necessary to remain competitive in today's dynamic global business environment. Employee empowerment is necessary if an organization is to have a committed, productive workforce.

Both the UAW and Rockwell agreed that this type of workforce would be mutually beneficial. The challenge for the negotiations team became how to achieve a productive relationship between labor and management. As with many successful change processes, change began with the leaders of both organizations. Options for traditional negotiations were explored and discussed. Both parties were searching for a way to fundamentally change the negotiation process so that both could work together to agree on a mutually beneficial contract. The UAW and Rockwell expressed a willingness to explore a partnership approach. This approach requires building trust and learning to jointly solve problems.

Background

A problem-solving, high-performance team-building process formed the cornerstone of the partnership approach to negotiations. The essence of this process is learning and implementing problem-solving and team-building processes learned at timed intervals throughout the negotiations.

The new approach represented a shift from the traditional presentation of demands, confrontational atmosphere, polarizing positions, and win-lose mentality. In contrast, the partnership approach is issue-oriented; problems are discussed, and conflict is managed to attain a win-win solution. Many obstacles had to be overcome to make this process effective, including putting aside experience, building trust, and attaining buy-in from negotiating members.

Successful accomplishment of this new negotiation process required support from UAW and Rockwell leadership, negotiating teams, and facilitators. Members of the teams were willing to risk leaving familiar roles and relationships to pursue an entirely different process. I was one of the program designers who implemented the process through high-performance team building and bargaining sub-committee interventions with a UAW Consultant and a Director of Organization Development for Rocketdyne. This team initiated the fundamental framework for the problem-solving, issues-oriented approach, and trust-building exercises.

Negotiation Process

Contract negotiations began in February 1990 in San Diego, California, with both sides agreeing that presentations of demands would be replaced by the presentation of issues and problems to be solved. This commitment to a new approach generated a positive climate as the traditional confrontational mode began to be displaced.

The negotiations convened for one week in April and began with one and a half days of highly interactive, high-performance team-building processes for the entire sixty-member Rockwell/UAW negotiating team. Participants were divided into groups who would work together to solve problems during the actual negotiations. The facilitators focused on frameworks and skills that would assist teams in building a climate of trust, open communication, appreciation of differences, and mutual respect. Members also learned techniques to increase information flow and analysis, manage conflict constructively, and maintain a win-win approach. Experiential exercises, skills training, and discussion were among several ways these goals were achieved.

One issue addressed initially was the need to leave past experiences behind so that a different approach to negotiations could be explored. All members present had the experience of using traditional bargaining tactics (e.g., threats, demands, emotionalism, "red herrings") to advance the goals of their organization. It was imperative now, however, to resist the temptation to resort to past win/lose tactics to achieve success and assume a learning posture towards the partnership approach. The old knowledge and behavior had to be replaced for the new approach to be successful. Effective communication and the risk of trust were areas Rockwell and the union reassessed.

In the past, communication included the presentation of demands. Very little listening took place as each side presented their lists in an uncompromising manner. Members listened for "flaws" instead of understanding. To work together productively, both sides learned that effective groups are those who share information openly, listen to one another, and provide feedback to members. As members open communication channels, trust can be developed. Management styles that allowed participants to identify alternatives to win/lose solutions were also discussed. For example, consensual decision-making does not produce winners and losers, as does a vote-driven process. Traditional negotiations reinforced the belief that if one side wins, the other loses—negotiators either are giving or getting. Negotiators learned that there are alternatives to this type of style. If communication is improved and based on openness, it becomes easier to obtain solutions that both sides consider acceptable.

Another exercise involved small group discussion around the characteristics of traditional labor negotiations and an issue-oriented, problem-solving approach. Some interesting differences between the two methods emerged when the small groups reported to the larger group. There was general agreement that traditional labor discussions were marked by a lack of trust and respect, inflexible and fixed positions, and a focus on demands. On the other hand, the new approach was described by the UAW/Rockwell teams as engendering trust, openness, teamwork, compromise, and a willingness to risk and change.

The two approaches are antithetical, and the latter is an entirely unfamiliar way to approach labor negotiations. The new approach required members to take risks. The negotiating group had to let go of familiar (and often perceived successful) methods of "winning" at the other's expense to make room for new skills and experiences.

During the discussion, facilitators asked negotiators to identify tactics and games they used to exercise power in previous negotiations. By exposing these methods, members rendered them ineffective. The information no longer held the influence it did when the knowledge was withheld. Now that everyone knew the tactics, it became possible during negotiations to stop their use by simply identifying the tactic being used.

Lack of trust between union and management members continued to be an important issue addressed during the educational process. Because of many adversarial experiences in the past, participants had to learn how to create and maintain trust and work as a single cooperative team. The union and management teams needed to thoroughly understand mutual trust and its benefits to begin to build a cooperative atmosphere among members. In a series of workshops, UAW and Rockwell members explored what trust meant to their relationship and what the consequences are when trust is violated.

Negotiating members gained insight into a dynamic in which the assumption was made that they were being lied to. There was now distance enough from this dynamic to enable union members to ask, "Can we believe them?" when management says they cannot afford something. Now management could question, "Is that true?" when the union replies that members will not accept something. In previous negotiations, the answers were assumed to be negative since a win/lose mentality was accepted. The message that became clear to negotiators was that success develops from cooperation; the success of one party is a prerequisite for the other party to do well.

Another important area addressed during labor discussions was conflict resolution. In past negotiations, proactive conflict resolution did not exist and could have been construed as a weakness. The rule in the past was not to "back down" or "give in." Now, productive resolution of differences is seen as imperative for effective communication. The facilitators led discussions about conflict resolution strategies, stressing the fact that people resolve differences in various ways. When communication channels are open, trust is apparent, and parties listen to each other, conflicts are resolved most effectively. Cooperation was an unfamiliar way for negotiators to resolve conflict, given the adversarial, competing manner utilized in the past.

Team problem-solving is another skill not used in traditional negotiations. To illustrate the benefits of group problem-solving and decision-making, facilitators presented an exercise that demonstrated that problem-solving groups make more informed, effective decisions than any one individual. This experience allowed negotiators to see that whether UAW or Rockwell, all members are resources who can provide knowledgeable information about problems to be solved for the mutual benefit of both.

Throughout the training, there were discussions focused on how these experiences would assist in the negotiation process. During negotiations, facilitators were present to provide consultation to the bargaining sub-committees to continually support the application of new skills.

One part of planning for negotiations was to determine, as a group, the guiding principles of an effective issue-oriented, problem-resolution approach to labor negotiations. Members of the team arrived at the following operating principles to guide the negotiation process: trust, mutual respect, open communication, shared objectives, and cooperation. These principles were to serve as the criteria by which to measure the progress of future discussions. These were also perceived as "givens" for the new approach to be successful. This process further helped negotiators establish a common language and foster trust through the creation of principles that all members agreed were necessary.

During the negotiation meetings, it sometimes proved useful to clarify Master Contract issues before trying to resolve them. One way in which this clarity was achieved was through role reversal, an activity that helped UAW members experience Rockwell's perceptions of the issues and vice versa. Members were asked to discuss and present issues and needs as if they were members of the other group. This allowed the two groups not only to understand how they are perceived by others but also to gain insight into the perspective and dilemmas facing the other group. Negotiating members profited from this exercise since the goal was simply to increase understanding, not to solve the issues being presented. Therefore, members were able to hear one another more clearly. Rockwell and the UAW were now able to assess whether each was well-informed enough about the other's issues to be a partner in problem-solving.

Second Negotiating Session

The second session of negotiations was held in May. Consistent with the first session, a workshop was conducted prior to the negotiating sessions. Part of the workshop consisted of re-establishing the guiding principles, reviewing the problem-solving approach, and renewing discussion about issues of trust, openness, and effective teams.

A portion of the day was devoted to returning to the discussion focused on the intellectual and behavioral differences between the traditional and issue-oriented approaches. Once the differences were laid out, the need to work, think, and act differently was addressed. Achieving successful outcomes required members to alter their previous views of labor negotiations.

The concept of paradigms was introduced by the facilitators to discuss why change is difficult. The group learned that a paradigm is a fixed framework or lens through which individuals view the world. Generally, paradigms are inflexible because they are bound by a person's experience and what is familiar to him/her. It is a paradox of paradigms that one must be willing to let go of previous knowledge and experience to gain new knowledge and experience. This was especially true when using a partnership instead of a traditional approach to negotiations. A paradigm shift is not simply adding to one's base of skills; it is a dramatic shift to new and unfamiliar territory.

The negotiators were able to understand that each member must fundamentally change his or her outlook of a union/management relationship; the old ways were seen as ineffective. When a paradigm shift occurs, everyone's skills go back to zero. As a result, changing paradigms is an uncomfortable process, and anxiety, frustration, and confusion are normal responses.

Awareness is necessary to increase understanding and enact change. This applies not only to paradigms but also to differences in perceptions, experience, and individual preferences that can have an impact on team functioning and outcomes. The facilitators pointed out that differences are important to gain all versions of the truth. The group worked on understanding the nature of individual differences and preferences in interaction and decision-making. This was another framework for members to learn about themselves and others in the group. The result of this learning was the importance of managing differences and utilizing different perspectives to derive creative and often unseen alternatives to problems and issues.

Third Session – Model the Behavior

The third session of training and negotiations took place in June for three consecutive weeks. Key issues were reviewed and discussed to allow members to reconnect with the team-building process. Initial training was given in a one-day session by the team of facilitators and focused on the management of meetings and techniques for effective communication, both critical skills for a team-oriented, problem-solving approach.

The consultation team outlined the technical requirements for holding a productive meeting. Union/Management subcommittees learned how to better plan the contents of meetings for joint goal attainment. The requirements presented pointed to planning successful meetings by outlining clear goals, structure, time frames, and participants. Besides managing content, negotiators also learned the importance of managing the process of a meeting. They discovered the implications of limited participation and the effect that domination by a few members can have on group communication. Negotiators discovered that open communication and full participation create a more effective team. Members learned to critique their own meeting process by identifying barriers to progress and taking appropriate action so that the issue-oriented, problem-solving approach could continue, and joint goals could be achieved.

Another skill necessary for effective team functioning is active listening. Traditionally, negotiators' primary concern was the demands they presented. The time in which the opposite group presented was a time to think of refutes to what they were hearing. This is counterproductive behavior for a high-performance team. Individuals learned how to listen in a way that ensured that what the speaker said was the same as what the listener heard. Paraphrasing, reflecting, questioning for clarification, and building on the statements of the speaker are all components of active listening implemented by the negotiating team.

Communication was again addressed, and negotiators learned how to give and receive feedback, discovered the impact of verbal and non-verbal messages, and discussed how self-fulfilling prophecies can be enacted. Each of these issues has a positive and negative side and can impact team communication in a constructive or destructive manner. For example, a self-fulfilling prophecy can be either "This process is definitely going to work" or "This new approach is useless." UAW and Rockwell members learned how to use these aspects of communication to enhance their functioning. High-performance teams are those that have clear goals, listen to one another, share responsibility for decisions, and freely give and receive constructive criticism. The union/management team is in the process of becoming such a team.

In the third week of June, close to the contract deadline, the negotiating teams were making progress. However, there was a need to focus on generating creative alternatives in order to break with the past. A decision was made by the facilitating team to conduct another half-day of joint, high-performance team building. In this session, teams described the processes they used during their negotiation meetings. Each sub-team outlined what their meetings were effective and ineffective. It became clear that using a problem-solving, issue-oriented approach set the stage for creative, innovative, non-traditional solutions to issues under negotiation. It was also apparent that teams utilizing this approach came up with better, mutually satisfying results than the other teams.

After a tentative agreement was reached by the UAW and Rockwell management, a final half-day was conducted to process the entire negotiating experience. Discussion centered around those aspects of the negotiations that assisted members in working effectively, those that prevented productive problem-solving, and those that members would change to improve UAW and Rockwell's work together.

Time was spent in this final session discussing how to continue this process back in the work environment. One solution to be implemented is similar training for management and union employees within the division. Additionally, an "Employee Involvement Philosophy" was jointly developed that emphasizes the importance of a partnership, mutual trust, and commitment to employees as the means to satisfy the shared goals of the company and the union. The philosophy that was agreed upon was followed the contract was ratified.

The success of the partnership approach to negotiations can be attributed to several factors. The essence of this approach was the learning and application of joint union/management cooperative team-building processes at intervals throughout the negotiations. Beyond this framework, several factors contributed to the success of the process:

- Joint management and union leadership with influence over the total negotiating group.
- Individuals from both sides were willing to take risks.
- Desire, initially, on the part of some participants to do negotiations differently, while others joined along the way.

- A theory and process for "win-win" versus "win-lose" negotiations and an alternative approach to traditional, adversarial approaches.
- Meeting of the entire negotiating team to receive feedback on progress from each of the bargaining sub-committees.
- Timed interventions that were planned and implemented with the total negotiating team throughout negotiations to increase the probability of influencing the group to continue the movement toward the achievement of the joint UAW/Rockwell goals.
- Trusted process facilitators who brought credibility and skills to the effort.

The goal of continuing a problem-solving approach on a day-to-day basis is that union/management negotiations could eventually be seen as a formality. That is, by the time the contract is renewed in three years, all problems and needs will have already been presented, discussed, and solved by the union and Rockwell members. The contract would simply be signed by both parties, reaffirming the agreements that had been reached on an ongoing basis.

Rockwell and UAW members took a risk. They chose to venture onto unfamiliar ground and face the anxiety that comes with the unknown. The negotiating team struggled to see its current paradigm and pushed further to create a new one to allow for change. The risk was met by unparalleled success—a joint negotiating team who walked away from the bargaining table fully satisfied and committed to an ongoing partnership relationship. This partnership between the UAW and Rockwell continued to thrive, and it still thrives with the Boeing Corporation, which acquired the aerospace and defense businesses.

Sharing my experiences in Rockwell as an internal organization change agent has been a learning experience for me. In writing this book, "It always seems impossible until it's done." – Nelson Mandela. It is a great feeling of accomplishment when it is done. A labor of love.

APPENDIX B
ROCKETDYNE DIVISION RESEARCH STUDY

An Account Summary

Introduction

I found this research project to be well-written, informative, and supportive of my work in changing organizations effectively. Dr. Olson did a fantastic job, and I am proud of her. She completed her internship with me at Rockwell.

A year after I guided the Rocketdyne Division through the Socio-Technical Systems Design Process (STS), a PhD student wrote her doctoral dissertation on the Rocketdyne division's change process. The research was conducted a year after Rocketdyne had completed the high-performance organization planning and design process, and the division was in the implementation phase of the process. The study was a quasi-longitudinal pre-test/post-test study with no control group, conducted at Rocketdyne Division in 1991.

Rocketdyne employed 10,000 people and had annual revenues of $1 billion. It manufactured the space shuttle main engines, delta rockets, lasers, and the space station power system.

This study measured changes in employee perceptions about the organization at Rocketdyne, which was undergoing significant change. At the time of the study, Rocketdyne was beginning its second year in a five-year process of redesigning its work systems from a traditional work structure to one based on sociotechnical principles. This intervention program and subsequent transition included analysis and change of the technical and social systems in the company to reach the goals of improving product quality, reducing costs, and meeting customer demands.

A validated survey instrument was used to assess the support and encouragement of six factors linked to organizations designed according to sociotechnical principles (Passmore, 1988). These factors included support for innovation, skills development, interaction with customers, cooperation among employees, organizational commitment, and joint optimization between people and technology. Passmore suggests that these factors distinguish between a traditionally designed organization and one designed according to sociotechnical principles.

Rocketdyne determined that their current structure, a functional-matrix design, was not effectively or efficiently meeting increasingly demanding customer and production goals. Changes were assessed using a quantifiable survey to identify what characteristics of the business were perceived to change due to the redesign.

Subjects were employees of Rocketdyne (pre-test n=103, post-test n=60). A group interview was conducted with Rocketdyne's organization members and the Human Resources department to gain further insight into the survey results.

The instrument used to measure the degree of change was the STS Assessment Survey, conceptualized by Passmore (1988) and further developed and validated by Sabiers (1992). Six survey factors are based on elements identified by Passmore that distinguish a traditional, bureaucratic organization from one designed based on sociotechnical principles.

The dimensions that Passmore suggests characterizing an organization based on STS theory design principles are support for a) innovation, b) human resource development, c) customer interface, d) cooperation, e) commitment to the organization, and f) joint optimization of people and technology. These correspond to the six dependent variables and survey factors tested in this study.

Based on STS theory and outcomes from other STS-based redesigns (Davis & Cherns, 1975; Emery & Trist, 1960; Passmore, 1988; Rice, 1958; Trist & Bamforth, 1951), it was hypothesized that each of these characteristics, except for joint optimization (identified as "Technical Efficacy" on the survey), would significantly increase from the pre-test to the post-test. It was predicted that the mean for the factor "Technical Efficacy" would remain the same from the first to the second testing.

The results of this study illustrate statistically significant increases for two of the six factors tested from the pre-test to the post-test, given approximately one year later. Each of the hypotheses was discussed, and alternate explanations of the results were explored. While not all factors showed statistically significant change, two outcomes achieved by Rocketdyne suggest that some positive change occurred at this organization.

Sociotechnical redesign is a resource-intensive process that can achieve flexibility in operations, responsiveness to the customer, and utilization of employees and technology to enhance a company's competitive edge. It appears that Rocketdyne may be on the right path and can now learn from both its successes and challenges in implementing STS design principles.

The business environment of the future promises only more chaos and uncertainty, requiring an adaptive organization that will decrease bureaucracy and increase internal cooperation (Dumaine, 1992). Changing business-as-usual is necessary to create this kind of organization. Though the present research has only limited significant results, the author supports the sociotechnical redesign theory and process as a viable method to accomplish deep-level, pervasive change.

APPENDIX C
THE DESIGN PHASES — THE BELLFLOWER HIGH SCHOOL

A Business/Education Partnership

PROFILES

Rockwell Corporation

Diversified, high-technology company

(Automation, avionics, aerospace, defense, electronics, telecommunications, automotive components, graphics systems)

Worldwide sales: $80 billion annually

Employees: 84,000 worldwide

Bellflower High School

Comprehensive high school, grades 7-12

Southeast Los Angeles County
Suburban/, lower middle-class

2400 students (Hispanic, white, African American, Asian

130 teachers and staff

This Account includes:

- The introduction and background to the organizational design process
- Bellflower High School background and rationale for selecting the school
- Overview of Bellflower Principal's role
- The partnership between Bellflower High and Rockwell
- Readiness and capability for school change and the case for change
- The importance of a systems approach to organizational change
- Today's Public Schools: Current Challenges and Needs
- The ten phases of the organizational design process implemented at Bellflower High

- The school design team and outcomes from the ten design phases
- Intangible side effects produced at Bellflower High as a result of the organizational design process
- Lessons learned from implementing the organizational design process
- Perspective on Rockwell Corporation and Bellflower High School: A Business/Education Partnership for the 21st Century
- Appendix (A) Bellflower Restructuring 21st Century Team

The design process is based on Socio-Technical Systems Theory (Cherns, 1976; Hann, 1988). It is an evidence-based business organizational design process. Walton (1980), supported by Galbraith and Lawler II (1993), indicated that the United States' command-and-control, bureaucratic, highly functional, industrial business model was broken, leaving customers and employees highly dissatisfied. A select number of U.S. businesses chose to use the Socio-Technical Systems design process to develop new competitive organizational paradigms. The intent was to use the design to increase competitiveness by providing customers with high-quality products and a motivated workforce.

This section will review the organizational design process developed and implemented at Bellflower High, resulting in a new school concept and design.

THE PHASES OF THE DESIGN PROCESS of the Bellflower High design process:

- Case for Change and Orientation to School Transformation
- Student Learning Outcomes and Values
- Curriculum
- Technology
- Analysis
- New School Concept and Design
- Implementation Planning
- Implementation
- Administration and "Staff Support Structure Design/Implementation
- Administrative Systems Design/Implementation

For the transformation to begin during the 1991-1992 school year at Bellflower High, it was critical to have a leader—the principal—who recognized the need for change, was willing to lead the change, and would work to assist the faculty, including key union leaders, in understanding the Case for Change.

The faculty generally agreed to initiate a large-scale school change process in December 1991, following four monthly faculty meetings and other discussions about the need to rethink the way students learn at Bellflower. During these meetings, a Case for Change was being built. The principal and faculty reviewed Bellflower High's student test scores, the SCANS report, and the National Goals for Education. By December, the faculty expressed, "We have been talking about the need for change since September; let's stop talking and get on with efforts to improve the school!"

However, some teachers argued that the problem lay with the students and parents, not the school. They believed, "They need to learn to adjust to our systems—it used to work; it's not our fault, it's the students." Despite these concerns, there was general agreement from a majority of the faculty to proceed. Teachers recognized that many of the instructional strategies, departmental silos, learning opportunities, and curriculum provided for students would not be sufficient for the 21st century.

An Orientation to the Change Process

Bellflower Faculty, Superintendent, Students, and Parents Meeting to Receive an Orientation to the Change Process

Once there was general faculty agreement to rethink the way education is provided at Bellflower High, the educational change consultant and Dr. Parker conducted an introduction and orientation to school transformation. This session was held in mid-January 1992, for all school faculty, students, and parents who could attend. Approximately 145 people, including the district superintendent, participated.

During the meeting, information was shared about why other schools were undergoing a transformation process, as well as details about the Bellflower High transformation design process. Several key principles guiding this process were explained:

1. **Self-Designed Process:** The school transformation design process is a self-designed, high-involvement process, to be completed by those responsible for the success of the school, including students, parents, and the community.
2. **Systemic Change:** The school is viewed as a system, and the intent from the beginning is to bring about systemic change in all key aspects of the school, driven by the student learning outcomes required in the 21st century.

The systems approach was contrasted with the "program of the month" approach to change, which tends to be short-lived, or a fragmented approach focusing on change in one grade level, testing area, subject, or section of the school at a time. The process was described as a journey, not an event. At the conclusion, all participants were invited to attend a day-and-a-half off-site school transformation meeting that would be conducted later in the month, addressing student learning outcomes and values, marking Phase II of the process.

Phase II Student Learning Outcomes/Values

Student Learning Outcomes The one and a half-day, off-site transformation meeting was conducted in late January 1992, on a Friday and Saturday, at Rockwell's Space Systems Division facility in Downey, California. This division builds the Space Shuttle and is located only a few miles from Bellflower High. Approximately 85 faculty, students, and parents attended. This meeting was designed to produce the first set of student learning outcomes and identify a set of values regarding student learning, curriculum, teachers, the school, administrators, the community, and the environment. The educational consultant and I facilitated this meeting. Rockwell paid a stipend to all Bellflower participants for Saturday, including students. The district provided substitute teachers for that Friday.

Three Sub-teams At the conclusion of this meeting, three sub-transformation design teams were formed to work over the next several months: one to conduct research and better identify the required student outcomes; another to work on the values; and the third to write a white paper describing the 21st-century societal context for the transformation (i.e., the social, cultural, economic, global, technological, and world-of-work characteristics). See Appendix F. The three transformation sub-teams worked between February and May 1992.

The sub-teams worked to get input from all the students and teachers, as well as as many parents as possible. To maximize student involvement, the sub-teams often used English classes since all students are required to take this course. Meetings were conducted with teachers during their conference periods to get their input and involve them. One of the sub-teams conducted a cable TV program to get parents and community involvement. All teachers gave their input, as well as approximately 1,100 students and a cross-section of parents.

This effort produced over 200 student learning outcomes, many values, and a "white paper" on 21st-century societal characteristics. The societal characteristics sub-team read literature and discussed a list of major trends observed by futurists in the fields of sociology, economics, family structure, demographics, and education. In part, they indicated that there is a growing trend towards national and global interdependence, a global economy, increasing change in both the pace and complexity of society, a "short half-life" of knowledge, the exploding growth of telecommunications and new materials, and a shift to an information and knowledge age with an emerging high-technology and service-based economy.

Results Shared at a Faculty Meeting The three transformation sub-teams presented the results of their work to a full faculty meeting, including a cross-section of students and parents, in June before the last day of school. There was general agreement and confirmation about the outcomes, values, and 21st-century societal context. The faculty was given the white paper on societal characteristics to read over the summer and think about the implications for the students, the school, curriculum, and existing instructional strategies and technology. The outcomes and values will be reviewed later.

Conference on Curriculum To maintain focus on the transformation process at Bellflower High over the summer, Rockwell supported a team from the school to attend an international education conference in August in Erie, Pennsylvania, on "Outcome-Based Curriculum for the 21st Century," sponsored by Joel Barker's EFG Curriculum Collaborative. This conference consisted of international teams of educators and business leaders collaborating to design a curriculum for the 21st century. The original structure of the EFG Curriculum Collaborative was designed by Joel Barker, a futurist and President of Infinity Limited, Inc. He and the educational change consultant assisting Rockwell with Bellflower's transformation process coordinated this international effort.

Bellflower's participation in this and another curriculum conference was financially supported by Rockwell.

International Education Conference on Curriculum In the summer, a large Bellflower team and the Rockwell change executive attended another session of the EFG Curriculum Collaborative International Education Conference on curriculum for the 21st century, held in Yorkshire, United Kingdom. The Bellflower team again shared the status of the transformation process. In this presentation, unlike the one in Erie, Pennsylvania, the Bellflower team gave the entire presentation.

The team also learned more about outcome-based curriculum development. During this conference, the Bellflower team was informed that a new superintendent had been appointed for the district. She was an extremely strong supporter of the Bellflower transformation design process.

The results of this conference opened an opportunity to move to the next phase of the transformation process, addressing the curriculum.

PHASE III CURRICULUM

Cross-Grade, Cross-Curricula Planning Teams In September, at the start of the 1992-1993 school year, Phase III of the transformation process addressed the curriculum through the formation of cross-grade, cross-curricula teams. This phase started with a full faculty meeting in September, including students and several parents. There were over 145 attendees.

The meeting was planned by the teachers who attended the conference, the principal, the education consultant, and the Rockwell change executive. Four major activities were planned and accomplished. First, results from the International Conference in Erie were shared, including teaching the faculty the curriculum development template learned at the conference for developing outcome-based curriculum. Second, the set of desired student learning outcomes/competencies identified in the prior school year (over 200 outcomes) were consolidated over the summer into six major topic areas and shared. They are:

- **Student Outcome 1: Speaking, Reading, Writing, Technological Skills**
  The learner will demonstrate competency in communication skills, including reading, writing, speaking, listening, producing quality work, and utilizing technology and multimedia.**Student Outcome 2: Preparedness for the World-Of-Work**
  The learner will prepare a plan and possess the skills for their future career, including managing time, working in teams, relating with co-workers, developing organizational skills, applying for jobs, developing resumes, and understanding business ethics.

- **Student Outcome 3: Civic Responsibility, History, Understanding the World**
  The learner will demonstrate competency in social studies, including geography, history, and economics, and will demonstrate a cultural and economic understanding of our global society.

- **Student Outcome 4: Knowledge of the Sciences, Including Awareness of Ecology and the Environment**
  The learner will demonstrate competency in physical, biological, and environmental sciences and understand local and global environmental issues in daily life.

- **Student Outcome 5: Higher Level of Math and Practical Application of Those Skills**
  The learner will demonstrate competency in higher-level math skills and apply these skills to business and personal experiences, including a critical analysis of real-life financial issues and their responsibilities.

- **Student Outcome 6: Healthy Living and Personal Responsibility**
  The learner will demonstrate an understanding of health, wellness, ethical behavior, and personal responsibility for him/herself.

Third, the values developed last school year were also consolidated, shared, and accepted as a set to guide the transformation process and behavior in the school. They are:

Values

- We value our staff as facilitators of learning who utilize multiple teaching strategies.
- We value a safe campus.
- We value a clean campus.
- We value a school atmosphere with mutual trust and respect for everyone.
- We value a school partnership of students, staff, parents, and community working cooperatively to ensure the mutual success of all.
- We value each staff member as a professional team member to ensure the educational success of all students.
- We value the school as an institution of the future, which motivates students to succeed.
- We value the physical, emotional, and mental well-being of our students, staff, and community.
- We value and respect the cultural diversities in our students and community.
- We value each student's uniqueness and individual ability to learn and succeed.
- We value each student's own participation and responsibility in the learning process.

Finally, six cross-grade, cross-subject teams of faculty, students, and parents were formed during the meeting. Each team was assigned one of the major consolidated sets of student outcomes and applied the curriculum development template they were taught. The goal was to involve everyone, so the teams averaged thirty members each, including faculty and students, and were open to parent involvement. Getting parent involvement was a difficult task and remained so throughout this process.

Curriculum Development Template In this meeting, each team practiced using the curriculum development template for their set of consolidated outcomes:

- Is it really a required learning outcome for the 21st century?
- Conduct research about the outcome.
- Identify where and how it is being taught at Bellflower, if at all.
- Identify a variety of student learning experiences based on the outcomes.
- Identify evaluation and assessment tools to measure learner competency.
- Determine where the outcomes should be taught, by whom, and the locations (grade levels, classrooms, individual or team of staff members, etc.).

At the conclusion of this meeting, each team provided the status of their work. The teams continued their work after the meeting in preparation for the October faculty transformation meeting.

They indicated that changes were likely required in the curriculum, the way classes are scheduled, the grouping of teachers and students, teachers' planning time, and instructional strategies if students are to learn the type of outcomes/competencies they had identified. At this point, some teachers began to see the possibilities of a new way that Bellflower could provide learning opportunities for students. The six teams continued their work and shared the results in the November and December faculty transformation meetings.

An important shift began to occur at this point in the process. Several highly respected informal leaders among the teachers started to assume responsibility for assisting the teams between the faculty meetings with facilitating curriculum development and planning for the transformation faculty meetings.

Applied Learning A curriculum development team working on one of the sets of student outcomes, "higher level of math and practical application of those skills," was interested in immediately improving the math curriculum to be more applied-student-learning-oriented. An engineer from Rockwell's Space Systems Division began assisting the Bellflower math department in October. They worked with him to develop applied math problems for students using issues related to the space shuttle. Also, to provide more applied learning for students in business education, a student field trip was organized to the Space Systems Division for approximately 60 Bellflower business education students.

This realization and view opened an opportunity to move the process to the next two phases: analysis and new school design.

PHASE III ANALYSIS

Analyze Innovative Schools

In this phase, the analysis focused on two areas: analyzing innovative schools with outcome/competency-driven curricula and examining how Bellflower High currently operated in the context of achieving the desired student outcomes/competencies.

In January, five innovative schools were identified and contacted by the education consultant. After agreements were reached, the five outcome teams met to plan the visits and to select 3-4 delegates from their teams, including students, to visit the schools. Special permission was granted by the School District to allow students to travel as team members. The schools were selected and matched with the teams based on the student outcomes that each team was addressing in curriculum development.

In February, the education consultant provided training to the teams on what to look for, the questions to ask, and how to best analyze the schools they were to visit. The visits and analyses were designed to expand their view of what was possible in a new school design. However, they were cautioned not to "cherry-pick" ideas for implementation at Bellflower High because the school needed to develop its own comprehensive design rather than taking a fragmented approach by selecting parts of what seemed to work at other schools. Visits and analyses took place in late February and March, with Rockwell covering all expenses for the teams that traveled across the country to visit the five schools.

The five schools selected and visited are described below, along with their exemplary qualities:

- **Sir Francis Drake High School**
  - *Location*: Tamalpais Union High School District, 1327 Sir Francis Drake Boulevard, San Anselmo, CA 94960
  - *Exemplary Qualities*: Integrated, rigorous curriculum in science, mathematics, English, social studies, technology, and the arts. They use technology-based learning, problem-solving groups, and virtual communities through networks. New assessment measures are used, and they have partnerships with parents, businesses, and colleges. They are redefining the role of the teacher and have an extended day and year.

- **Mt. Edgecumbe High School**
  - *Location*: 1330 Seward Ave., Sitka, Alaska 99835
  - *Exemplary Qualities*: Prepares students for the world of work by having a company within the school, utilizing authentic assessments and technology. The school also uses quality processes, alternative schedules, group and teamwork, problem-solving, and responsibility.
- **Horace Mann Middle School and International High School**
  - *Location*: 3351 23rd Street, San Francisco, CA 94110
  - *Exemplary Qualities*: Integrated instruction, use of technology, block scheduling, team approach, problem-solving, and urban setting.
- **Wasson High School**
  - *Location*: Colorado Springs, Colorado
  - *Exemplary Qualities*: Transforming for the 21st century by using integrated instruction, alternative scheduling, etc. Featured on Tom Brokaw's network news, with visitors from across the nation.
- **Bravo Middle School**
  - *Location*: Bloomington, Minnesota
  - *Exemplary Qualities*: Utilizes alternative schedules, team approach, integrated instruction, problem-solving, and is outcome-based.

Results Shared

In late March, the visiting teams shared their analyses and learnings with the other team members and faculty who were not part of the visits. There was a great deal of excitement at this point. The education consultant and Rockwell change executive were present at these meetings, assisting with facilitating the sharing and learning. They again suggested that the staff avoid cherry-picking concepts from the schools they visited when designing the new Bellflower High School, but rather use the results of their analyses as data to inform what would be the best new school design for Bellflower High. However, it was appropriate for interested teachers to take ideas they had learned and try them in their classrooms, and this was done.

After the students and teachers shared their visit experiences, the next step was to analyze Bellflower High in the context of the visit results and achieving the student outcomes/competencies. A transformation design team was formed, open to all. Forty faculty and students composed the team, many of whom had visited the innovative schools, in addition to other interested faculty members. Faculty members who were unable to participate on the design team were strongly encouraged to give their ideas to this team.

Key Learnings from the Analysis

- It was confirmed that the way Bellflower's current educational system was structured made it extremely difficult for students to learn the desired student outcomes.
- The predominant instructional strategy was teacher-centered, lecture-based, with students being mostly passive learners and not actively engaged in their own learning.
- Students in Grades 7-12 experienced subjects by grade vertically with little to no coordination and integration horizontally across subjects.
- There was general recognition by both sub-teams, with only one or two member exceptions, that a new school design was needed.

PHASE IV NEW SCHOOL CONCEPT AND DESIGN

Sub Teams of the Design Team

In this phase of the transformation process, each sub-team of the design team was tasked with independently developing a new school design for Bellflower High that would facilitate the achievement of the desired student outcomes and values. They were also instructed to incorporate insights from the curriculum development experience and the analysis of innovative schools. The purpose of having two sub-teams was to generate two different school designs that the design team could later evaluate.

The two sub-design teams worked separately for several weeks to develop their respective school designs. Once both designs were completed, the teams came together to share their ideas. After this sharing session, the two sub-design teams were merged into a single team. This newly formed team was tasked with synthesizing the best elements from both sub-teams' work to design the optimal school for Bellflower High. They were encouraged to think creatively and not be limited by the initial designs. The team was expected to complete their work and present the new school design to the entire faculty for approval in May.

After weeks of debate, frustration, brainstorming, and disagreements, the design team successfully developed a new school design by the end of May. Once the design was finalized, the team began working on creating a new school schedule that would support the new school design. However, after much hard and frustrating work, the design team concluded that they were not yet ready to present both the new school design and the supporting schedule to the faculty. Instead, they decided to present the overarching concepts of the new school design, particularly the commonalities that had emerged from their discussions. The team recognized that more time was needed to develop a comprehensive class schedule. The education consultant and the Rockwell change executive facilitated many of these design team meetings.

New School Concept Shared with Faculty

The design team shared the new school concept with all faculty members in small meetings during their conference periods to maximize faculty input. The proposed concept described to the faculty was centered on a student-focused, outcome-driven curriculum. In this concept, students would select a major from a proposed set of seven major areas, supported by thematic or project-oriented integrated courses taught by cross-grade, cross-curricula teaching teams. The career paths team, which had been working in parallel with the school transformation process, had previously identified the seven major areas: Industrial Technology/Manufacturing, Business, Environmental, Health/ Home Recreation, Performing Arts, Visual Arts, and Social/Human Services. Upon graduation, students would receive a diploma as well as a certificate certifying the completion of a major.

For example, students selecting a major in social/human services would engage in projects such as operating a U.S. travel agency. This applied, active learning would involve related courses in math, English, business, and social studies, all taught by a team of teachers in a three-hour block of time. This is referred to as a "cluster," which supports a major. A cluster is a grouping of 2-4 courses in different subject areas, encompassing a given block of time and revolving around a theme or project. Students would have significant flexibility in choosing their majors until the eleventh grade, allowing them to explore their interests before making a final selection. An example of this cluster concept is shown below.

SAMPLE CLUSTER CONCEPT:

MAJOR: SOCIAL / HUMAN SERVICES

PROJECT: U.S. TRAVEL AGENCY

RELATED COURSES TEAM TAUGHT:

MATH, ENGLISH, BUSINESS, SOCIAL STUDIES

Students

In this concept, students would demonstrate competencies through authentic assessment, using a competency checklist for each set of outcomes. They would complete the core required state academics, actively participate in learning, and benefit from block flexible scheduling with support from advisors, parents, mentors, and the community.

For example, a competency checklist for one of the sets of outcomes/competencies might include:

- Demonstrate competency in social studies, including geography, history, and economics.
- Demonstrate cultural understanding of our global society.
- Demonstrate economic understanding of our global society.

Teachers

In this concept, teachers would select a major in an area of interest, act as facilitators of learning, team-teach within a cluster, and adopt a cross-curricular, integrated approach to instruction. They would also have a shared planning period to collaborate effectively.

PHASE V NEW SCHOOL SCHEDULE DESIGN

The new schedule sub-team was unable to recommend a specific schedule after two days of deliberation but was able to agree on the fifteen "MUSTS" for the new schedule:

1. Must facilitate meeting the student learning outcomes/competencies.
2. Must allow for a variety of learning activities.
3. Must have flexible hours for learning activities.
4. Length of periods must be expanded.
5. Must identify the number of classes each day.
6. Must identify which day of the week classes will meet.
7. Must include common planning periods.
8. Must meet student and community needs, including LEP, remediation, transiency, newcomer, and co-curricular activities.
9. Must consider the number of teacher preparations per day, with fewer preparations preferred.
10. Must lower the teacher/student ratio per day.
11. Must accommodate a variety of methods for grouping students.
12. Does not mandate single grade-level grouping.
13. Parenting skills need to be integrated into the curriculum.
14. Remediation must be included within the school day.
15. Employment during the regular day should be tied to ROP (community growth).

16. Must configure a schedule that offers "choices."
17. Must support Advanced Placement (AP) classes.
18. Must support a seventh-grade foundation program.
19. Must keep the schedule simple.

Both sub-teams presented their recommendations to the full team at the conclusion of the meeting on Saturday and reached a consensus. There was also agreement to modify the current class schedule where possible to allow several teams of teachers to pilot their project clusters and integrated teaching approach. The new schedule sub-team agreed to continue researching ways to design a new class schedule that meets the 15 "MUSTS."

The new superintendent attended the Saturday meeting, listened to the sub-team reports, was extremely supportive, and encouraged continued work. The Rockwell change executive and the education consultant assisted with facilitating this meeting, and Rockwell provided refreshments and food at the community center.

In January, the principal of Bellflower High retired, and a new principal was appointed in February.

Next Design Team Meeting

The next design team meeting was held in March for two days at the Bellflower School District office. It was a Friday and Saturday meeting open to everyone interested. The new principal attended as a member of the design team, along with approximately 40 team members.

The primary objective of the meeting was to design a new class schedule that meets the 15 "MUSTS" identified by the sub-team in December. Before starting this work, however, the design team reviewed the status and progress of several teams of teachers who were implementing the project-oriented cluster approach to instruction and examined the implications for a new school schedule. The teachers were excited about their work, as were some of the students who participated in this approach to learning. The teachers emphasized the value of team teaching, integrated courses, a flexible schedule, and the need for common planning time as well as an increase in planning time. The design team was encouraged by the students' positive reactions to this different way of learning.

The results of a student survey were also shared, indicating that students supported the cluster concept and suggested the following clusters:

Swimming	Custom Design	Barber Shop
Comics	Bank	Coffee Shop
Toy Shop	Hobby Shop	Engineering
Restaurant	Book Shop	ROTC
Self Defense	Bike Shop	Modeling
Fashion Design	Silk Screening	Biology
Radio Station	Mini-Mall	Accounting
Photo Class	Air Brushing	Community Talent Show
Psychology	Physical Therapy	Greenhouse
Dance Hall	Day Care	Law Enforcement
Television Company	Candy Shop	Chiropractor
Real Estate	Pre-school	Zoology
Translator		

After these reports, the design team spent the remaining time developing a flexible class schedule to meet the "MUSTS." After sharing research and school visit results, engaging in debate and discussion, the design team was surprised to reach a consensus on a new school block schedule by the end of the first day. The second day was spent resolving the scheduling issues that had to be overcome for implementation.

They also identified potential concerns teachers might raise about the new schedule, prepared responses, and strategized how to present the new schedule to the full faculty for consensus. The new principal actively participated and provided tremendous support for the transformation process, the new school design, and the schedule. The Rockwell change executive assisted in facilitating this meeting, with the primary work done by the design team members. Rockwell provided food and refreshments.

Presentation to Faculty

In early April, a representative group of design team members presented the new class schedule to the faculty in small groups during their conference periods over two days. They began presenting at 6:30 a.m. for those who wanted to be briefed outside of their conference period. The team was well-prepared for these meetings, presenting five variations of the recommended block schedule, outlining the benefits to students and teachers, and answering tough questions.

The five variations of the proposed schedule included:

- An eighth-grade block schedule with a U.S. Travel Agency project cluster,
- A ninth-grade advanced student block schedule,
- A tenth-grade manufacturing major with supporting cluster schedule,
- An eleventh-grade advanced placement block schedule, and
- A twelfth-grade regular block schedule.

The greatest resistance and disagreements came from the coaching staff, performing arts faculty, and a few faculty members who chose not to be involved in the transformation design process.

New Proposed Schedule

The new proposed block class schedule features a traditional schedule of classes on Mondays with six periods but differs significantly on Tuesday-Thursday and Wednesday-Friday. On Monday, school starts at 6:30 a.m. with a zero period for band, drill team, or other courses of interest to students and teachers. This period is followed from 7:30 a.m. to 8:45 a.m. by a common teacher team planning time. The first regular period then starts at 8:45 a.m. and ends with the sixth period at 2:43 p.m., with regular fifty-minute periods. The school day ends with an activity period from 2:50 p.m. to 3:40 p.m.

The timing on Tuesday-Thursday and Wednesday-Friday follows the same pattern. On these days, school starts with a zero period from 6:30-7:25 a.m., followed by a tutorial period where all teachers are in their homerooms to assist students with problems they had with tests and assignments. On Tuesdays and Thursdays, periods 1, 3, and 5 are scheduled (each lasting approximately 1½ hours), ending with an activity period. On Wednesdays and Fridays, students attend periods 2, 4, and 6 (each also lasting approximately 1½ hours), again ending with an activity period.

Benefits for Students and Teachers

In the briefings to the faculty, the design team members explained the benefits of this new block schedule for students and teachers. These benefits include:

- More learning time for students,
- Fewer students per teacher each day,
- Fewer preparations per day (with the same instructional minutes),
- Weekly coordinated, school-wide planning times,
- More effective use of class time (reduced transitions),
- More uninterrupted time for teacher-student contact,

- Increased flexibility for a variety of teaching strategies,
- Opportunities for cooperative activities and group interaction,
- In-depth advanced placement discussion time,
- Mainstreaming of special needs students,
- Fewer opportunities for tardies,
- Less chance for conflict (fewer passing periods),
- No bells,
- Increased time for lab activities,
- Retention of single classes with a longer block of time, and
- More planning time and team-teaching strategies for teachers.

In contrast, the traditional schedule that this replaces has six periods starting at 7:45 a.m., each lasting approximately 55 minutes with ten-minute snacks and seven-minute passing times. The school day ends at 2:31 p.m. This traditional schedule primarily supports individual teachers teaching their subjects in individual classrooms.

Faculty Vote

After the new proposed schedule and its benefits were shared with the entire faculty in April, a full staff meeting was conducted a week later by the principal to discuss and vote on the proposed new schedule. Prior to the meeting, there was extensive discussion among the faculty about the pros and cons of the new block schedule, and the discussion continued during the meeting before the vote. The faculty conducted a secret vote at their request.

The results were inconclusive, with 50% supporting the new schedule and approximately 50% opposing it. The voting ballot allowed faculty to provide reasons for their support or opposition to the new schedule.

Changes in the Proposed Schedule Followed by Second Faculty Vote

The results were tabulated, and all the comments were organized and shared with the faculty. There were four teacher meetings in April following this vote, reviewing the reasons for support or opposition to the proposed schedule and discussing recommendations for improvement. These meetings were crucial, providing both supporting and opposing faculty the opportunity to participate and voice their opinions. Modifications were made to the new schedule based on the recommendations, and another faculty vote was taken on April 27, with a majority approving the modifications.

The changes included having three days—Monday, Wednesday, and Friday—with traditional 47 to 55-minute classes, with six periods, and two days—Tuesday and Thursday—with 1 hour and 40-minute period block schedules. The three-day class schedule would therefore have periods 1 through 6 approximately 47 minutes each on Mondays and 55 minutes on Wednesdays and Fridays.

There is still the zero period and common time for teacher/team planning and staff meetings. The proposed two-day block schedule (Tuesday and Thursday) starts with a zero period, followed by a tutorial time with periods 1, 2, and 3 each lasting 1 hour and 40 minutes, and on Thursday, the day starts the same but has periods 4, 5, and 6 lasting the same amount of time. This was the schedule proposed and voted on for the 1994-1995 school year (see Appendix C).

The results of this voting for the revised proposed block schedule for the 1994-1995 school year were as follows:

- 70% of staff favored the modified proposed block schedule,
- 15% of staff were neutral, and
- 15% of staff opposed it.

Next Steps

The next steps taken after a majority of the faculty supported the modified schedule included:

- The principal meeting with the Bellflower District Education Association Teacher Union's Negotiating Committee, who supported the modified block schedule, but it needed to be voted on by the union membership at Bellflower High.
- The principal met with the Superintendent's Council, who approved the new schedule.
- The principal and superintendent met with the school board, who also approved the new schedule.

Bellflower Education Association Union Vote

In June 1994, the proposed modified school schedule was put to a teacher's union membership vote and was defeated by one vote. In subsequent meetings, the modified schedule was further adjusted and brought to a final vote a week before the end of the school year in June. The modified schedule was defeated once again by two votes.

Many supporters were ineligible to vote because they had come during the second semester (January) and were temporary or long-term substitutes. Based on this experience, the district-level union leadership is considering provisions so that future school changes like this can be handled differently. Even with these results, some teachers continued with implementation planning over the summer.

PHASE VII IMPLEMENTATION PLAN

Summer Implementation Planning and Implementation Steering Committee

During the summer, seven teams of teachers planned either project clusters, thematic units expandable to clusters, or core units. An eighth team focused on planning the seventh-grade core and cluster. These teams worked on implementing this part of the new school design for the 1994-1995 school year, starting in September, involving approximately 30 teachers. The administration collaborated with the teams to develop a new, flexible school schedule to support these initiatives.

All the concepts in the proposed new schedule, except for the advisory, tutorial, and school-wide planning time, remained intact. They also planned for the summer registration for the students. Planning was done in the following project clusters, core, and thematic units, indicating the length of time, grade(s), periods, teaching teams, and subjects.

Cores: One or two teachers combining two closely related subjects, such as English and Social Studies, taught in back-to-back classes with the same group of students, allowing for integrated efforts in some or all curriculum areas.

MANUFACTURING COMPANY (cluster; all year) – Grade 9, Periods 1,2,3

Mike Matheson	(711)	Industrial Technology
Linda Riccio	(608)	English
Katrina White	(903)	Applied Math
Project: Creation and marketing of a product		
Resource: Rockwell: Digital Communication Division, Allen-Bradley, Information Systems Center		

AMERICAN TRAVEL AGENCY (cluster; 1st semester) –Grade 8, Periods 1,2,3

Trish Farber	((310)	Pre-algebra; Advanced Pre-algebra
Darrenn Platt	(303)	Social Studies 8; Advanced Social Studies 8
Sue Rosenberg	(302)	English 8; Advanced English 8
Project: Travel and tourism in the United States.		

ENGLISH/WORD PROCESSING (cluster; all year) –Grade 12, Periods 1,2

Tom Hogan	(514)	Advance English 12
Kathy Stanger	(402/406)	Word Processing
Sue Rosenberg	(302)	English 8; Advanced English 8
Project: Using word processing, business English to improve writing.		

ENGLISH/SOCIAL STUDIES (core; all year) –Grade 9, Periods 3, 4

Elisa Hastings	(415)	English 9
Keith Landhan	((T4)	Social Studies 9
Project: English and social studies with drama and multicultural emphasis.		

WORLD TRAVEL AGENCY (Theme units; expandable to cluster) –Grade 11/12, Period 5

Shari Whitney	(402)	Computer Applications
Keith Landhan	((T4)	Social Studies 9
Project: Travel and tourism worldwide, with technology emphasis		

FITNESS ACADEMY (Theme units; expandable to cluster) –Grade 9, Period 1,3

Shari Whitney	(402)	Computer Applications
Cindy Rector	(PE)	Social Studies 9
Project: Long-term fitness/wellness planning		

FUTURES IN SPACE (cluster/team; 2nd semester) –Grade 8, Period 1, 2, 3

Farber, Platt, Rosenberg		
Ken Eslick	((701)	Industrial Technology 8
Project: Bellflowerites colonize Mars in 2050		
Resource: Rockwell Space Systems Division		

7TH GRADE CORE

Kathy	(304)
Jonathan	(907)
Sylvia	(901)
Cheryl	(908)
Jim	(902)
Eric	(307)
7th grade English/Social Studies program where one teacher has students for two consecutive periods and combines curriculum whenever possible.	

During the summer, four faculty members, including the new principal, attended another session of the EFG International Curriculum Collaborative Conference held in Chattanooga, Tennessee. The principal was immersed in discussions about integrated curriculum and returned with new ideas, particularly about implementation and the use of instructional technology.

PHASE VIII IMPLEMENTATION

In September 1994, the teams who planned during the summer began implementation, with the "Future in Space Cluster" scheduled for launch in January 1995, during the second semester. Preliminary results in early November from teachers working with approximately 250 students participating in this element of the new school design indicate that the students are achieving significantly better grades, have lower absenteeism, and experience fewer disciplinary problems.

In a full faculty planning meeting in late November, the faculty agreed to implement the total new school design, including the majors, the supporting cluster concept, and a review of the schedule. There were ten majors, including the seven identified earlier by the design team, as well as Math/Science/Engineering, Communications, and Liberal Arts majors. The majors will be introduced with students in an exploratory stage in their seventh and eighth grades, where they will receive career interest support, career assessments, and preparation for major/career interest areas.

All students in the ninth and tenth grades will receive career interest support and assessments and will work within an interest area leading to a major/career path. Students will be required to commit to a major in their junior year, with work placement and/or community service in either their junior or senior year, or both. This is still being determined. Each teacher will select a major they wish to advise. Every student in grades 9-12 will have a career path advisor, and every teacher, as well as other staff members, will have a group of students under their advisement. Additionally, each major/career path team of teachers will be networked with a community resource to provide support for the major and to offer more applied learning opportunities, such as partnerships with Rockwell, local community businesses, health organizations, environmental agencies, local theater groups, colleges, and universities.

During the second semester (beginning in January), new clusters and courses will be piloted. Teachers will likely serve as major advisors primarily for juniors and seniors this year, and pre-registration will focus on the majors, as well as clusters and classes needed to complete skills certificates within those majors. In revisiting the schedule and attempting to create and implement a master school schedule since September, it has become clear that a block schedule would be challenging to implement alongside the cluster system, so other alternatives and modifications are being considered.

The plan is to design the master school schedule between December 1994 and March 1995, with implementation in the 1995-1996 school year. The new school concept and design are outlined below.

The next two phases of the school transformation design process—Administration and "Staff" Support Systems Design, and Administrative Systems Design—have been partially changed and were in the process of being analyzed and redesigned to support the new school design.

PHASE IX ADMINISTRATION AND "STAFF" SUPPORT STRUCTURE

In the administration and "staff" support design phase, the roles and responsibilities of the principal, assistant principals, counselors, department chairs, and other teacher and student support systems are analyzed to determine the structural changes required to support the new school design. Site-based management and how it will function at the school become part of this phase of the transformation planning process.

This area was partially addressed in the summer of 1994. The principal, in consultation with the transformation implementation steering team, modified the roles of the assistant principals and counselors to better support the emerging new school design. The department chairs' roles, along with other key staff support functions, are currently under study.

PHASE X ADMINISTRATIVE SYSTEMS DESIGN

In the administrative systems design phase, the recruitment, selection, orientation, and staff development systems are analyzed and modified to support the new design. Additionally, the communication, information, instructional technology, and reward and recognition systems are also updated.

To support the emerging new school design, the faculty recruitment and selection process was partially revised in March 1993 by the design team with the support of the superintendent. The team collaborated with the school district to develop a teacher interview process aimed at identifying and selecting teachers who had a propensity for working successfully in teams and within the new school design. This effort was in anticipation of many teachers retiring at the end of the school year due to retirement incentives. Thirty new teachers were hired through this process.

Furthermore, in June, at the end of the school year, the education consultant conducted an in-service staff development training session for existing Bellflower High teachers, focused on the skills required in the new school design. Additional staff development training is planned by the implementation steering committee, along with changes in other administrative systems.

Instructional Technology Support System for the New School Design

Rockwell's Information Systems Center continued to assist Bellflower High in planning the instructional technology support system required for the new school design.

The plan includes having a television and VCR in every classroom, one interactive Level III (or higher) laser disk player for every five classrooms, all classrooms cabled with head-in accessibility, a resource center with 30 computers (LAN) for research, careers, instructional applications, and 100-160 wings with student resource rooms consisting of 10 computers connected to LAN/Shared server.

Additionally, Rockwell is assisting Bellflower High in gaining early access to the Information Superhighway and Electronic Information via the Internet. The Information Systems Center is working with its vendors (GTE in particular) to help Bellflower achieve its instructional technology goals.

Role of Rockwell

Rockwell will work with the school to determine how it can best continue assisting Bellflower High as the new emerging school design evolves. Discussions are focused on Rockwell aiding the majors and supporting project clusters by forming partnerships between appropriate businesses and the teams of teachers responsible for the majors, thereby assisting with the school-to-work transition.

For instance, in the industrial technology and manufacturing major, this team of teachers has a partnership with several Rockwell businesses that will assist with the application of learning and provide student work internships. Rockwell is helping teachers with curriculum development and arranging teacher visits to Rockwell businesses such as Allen-Bradley in Milwaukee, WI, where there is a state-of-the-art manufacturing facility.

Rockwell's Information Systems Center is also collaborating with these teachers, as they are discussing the incorporation of various information technology tools and capabilities. Not only is the school looking at traditional areas of computer-aided design and manufacturing, but they are also exploring computer numerical control, laser technology, and robotics.

This new paradigm mandates discussions on team concepts and a process focus. Rockwell is helping the manufacturing major teachers understand the premise and advantages of the continuous improvement process as an adjunct to their normal curriculum. It may also be appropriate for some teachers and students to attend process improvement training programs conducted by Rockwell or attend other relevant training programs. Additionally, assistance is being provided in incorporating the new area of multimedia into teachers' instructional strategies.

The "Futures in Space" cluster of teachers has a partnership with Rockwell's Space Systems Division. The plan under consideration is for Rockwell to assist Bellflower in this way with the majors in the school and the supporting project clusters. When Rockwell is unable to provide direct assistance, it will help the school network with appropriate resources.

For example, Bellflower High has been introduced to representatives from UCLA's Graduate School of Education, who, after visiting Bellflower High in October 1994, have offered to assist with leadership training in managing large system changes in education and networking with other innovative schools in the Los Angeles area. Rockwell has also introduced Bellflower High to representatives from UCLA's School of Medicine, who have developed a method of teaching science and math that engages students through interactive computers.

This method also provides teachers with insights into how students think as they solve problems. After a demonstration to the principal and several teachers, there was interest on the part of Bellflower High because it supported outcomes-based learning and the emerging new school concept and design. A plan is being developed by UCLA to train Bellflower teachers in its use. The quality of the educational process that students experience will be greatly enhanced by fundamental structural changes in the design of schools, supported by the involvement of community resources.

***

REFERENCES

Argyris, C. (1964) Integrating the Individual and the Organization. New York: John Wiley.

Barko, W. & Passmore, W. (1986). Introductory statement to the special issue on sociotechnical systems: Innovations in Designing High-Performance Systems. *The Journal of Applied Behavioral Science, 22, 195-199.*

Beckard, R. & Harris, R.T. (1987). *Organizational Transitions* (2nd Ed.). Massachusetts: Addison Wesley.

Beekun, R.I. (1989). *Assessing the Effectiveness of Sociotechnical Interventions: Antidote or Fad? Human Relations,* 42 *(10), 877-897.*

Belgard, Fisher, Rayner, Inc. (1990). *High-Performance Systems (Training materials). Beaverton, OR: Author.*

Campbell, D.T. & Stanley, J.C. (1963). Experimental and Quasi-Experimental Designs for Research. Dallas: Houghton Mifflin.

Carlsmith, J.M., Ellsworth, P.C., & Aronson, E. (1976). *Methods of Research in Social Psychology.* New York: Random House.

Carnevale, A.P. (1991). *America and the New Economy.* Alexandria, VA: American Society for Training and Development.

Cherns, A. (1976). *The Principles of Sociotechnical Design. Human Relations,* 29 (8), 783-792.

Crano, W.D & Brewer, M.B. *Principles and Methods of Social Research.* Boston: Allyn and Bacon.

Cummings, T.G. (1978). *Sociotechnical Systems: An Intervention Strategy.* In W.A. Pasmore & J.J. Sherwood (Eds.*), Sociotechnical Systems: A Sourcebook* (pp. 168-187). La Jolla, CA: University Associates.

Davis, L.E. (1971a). *The Coming Crisis for Production Management: Technology and Organization. International Journal of Production Research*, 9(1), 65-82.

Davis, L.E. (1971b*). Job Satisfaction Research: The Post-Industrial View. Industrial Relations*, 10, 176-193.

Davis, L.E. (1979). Job Design: Historical Overview. In L.E. Davis & J.C. Taylor (Eds.), Design of Jobs (2nd Ed.) (pp. 29-35). Santa Monica: Goodyear.

Davis, L.E. & Cherns, A.B. (Eds.). (1975*). The Quality of Working Life, Volume Two: Cases and Commentary. New York: Free Press.*

Davis, L.E. & Taylor, J.C. (1975). *Technology Effects on Job, Work, and Organizational Structure: A contingency View. In L.E. Davis & A.B. Cherns (Eds.), The Quality of Working Life, Volume One (pp. 220-241). New York: Free Press.*

Davis, L.E. & Taylor J.C. (Eds.). (1979). *Design of Jobs (2nd Ed.).* Santa Monica: Goodyear.

Davis, L.E. & Taylor J.C. (Eds.). (1979*). Improving the Quality of Working Life: Sociotechnical Case Studies. In L.E. Davis & J.C. Taylor (Eds.), Design of Jobs (2nd Ed.)* (pp. 162-183). Santa Monica: Goodyear.

Dumaine, B. (1990, May). *Who Needs A Boss?* Fortune, pp. 52-60. Dumaine, B. (1991, June). *Bureaucracy Busters. Fortune*, pp.36-50.

Dyer, W.G. (1987). Team Building (2nd Ed.). Reading, MA: Addison-Wesley.

Emery, F.E. & Trist, E.L. (1960). Sociotechnical Systems. Sciences, Models, and Techniques, 2, 83-97.

Emery, F.E. & Trist, E.L. (1972). Towards a Social Ecology. London: Plenum Press.

Galagan, P. Work Teams That Work. (1986). Training and Development Journal, 11, 33-35.

Galbraith, J.R. (1973). Designing Complex Organizations. Reading: Addison-Wesley.

Galbraith, J.R. (1987). Organization Design. In J.W. Lorach (Ed.), <u>Handbook of Organizational Behavior</u> (pp. 343-357). Englewood Cliffs: Prentice Hall.

Guzzo, R.A., Jette, R.D., & Katzell, R.A. (1985). The Effects of Psychologically Based Intervention Programs on Worker Productivity: A Meta-Analysis. <u>Personnel Psychology</u>, <u>38</u>, 275-291.

Hackman, J.R. (1975). <u>Man and Work in Society</u>. New York: Van Nostrand-Reinhold.

Hackman, J.R. (1981). Sociotechnical Systems Theory: A Commentary. In A.H. Van de Ven & W.F. Joyce (Eds.), <u>Perspectives on Organizational Design and Behavior</u> (pp. 76-86). New York: John Wiley.

Hackman, J.R. (1983). Designing Work for Individuals and For Groups. In J.R. Hackman, E.E. Lawler III & L.W. Porter (Eds.), <u>Perspectives on Behavior in Organizations</u> (pp. 242-258). New York: McGraw Hill.

Hackman, J.R. (1986). The Psychology of Self-Management in Organizations. In M.S. Pallak & R.O. Perloff (Eds.), <u>Psychology and Work</u> (pp. 89-136). Washington D.C.: APA.

Hackman, J.R. & Lawler, E.E. (1971). Employee Reactions to Job Characteristics. <u>Journal of Applied Psychology Monograph</u>, <u>55</u>, 259-286.

Hackman, J.R. & Lawler, E.E. III (1979). Job Characteristics and Motivation: A Conceptual Framework. In L.E. Davis & J.C. Taylor (Eds.), <u>Design of Jobs</u> (2nd Ed.). (pp. 75-84). Santa Monica: Goodyear.

Hackman, J.R. & Oldham, G.R. (1975). Development of the Job Diagnostic Survey. <u>Journal of Applied Psychology</u>, <u>60</u>, 159-170.

Hackman, J.R. & Oldham, G.R. (1975). Motivation Through the Design of Work: Test of a Theory. <u>Organizational Behavior and Human Performance</u>, <u>16</u>, 250-279.

Hackman, J.R. & Oldham, G.R. (1980). <u>Work Redesign</u>. Reading, MA: Addison-Wesley.

Hanna, D.P. (1988). <u>Designing Organizations for High Performance</u>. New York: Addison-Wesley.

Herbst, P.G. (1974). <u>Sociotechnical Design</u>. London: Tavistock.

Herzberg, F.I., Mausner, B., & Snyderman, B.B. (1959). <u>The Motivation to Work</u>. New York: John Wiley.

Herzberg, F.I. (1966). <u>Work and The Nature of Man</u>. Cleveland: World.

Herzberg, F.I. (1968). One More Time: How Do You Motivate Employees? <u>Harvard Business Review</u>, Jan-Feb., 53-62.

Herzberg, F.I. (1979). Orthodox Job Enrichment. In L.E. Davis & J.C. Taylor (Eds.), <u>Design of Jobs</u> (2nd Ed.) (pp. 136-147). Santa Monica: Goodyear.

Hoerr, J. (1989, July). The Payoff From Teamwork. <u>Business Week</u>, pp. 56-62.Hulin, C.L. & Blood, M.R. (1968).

Job Enlargement, Individual Differences, and Worker Responses. <u>Psychological Bulletin</u>, <u>69</u>, 41-55.

Kanter, R.M. (1983). <u>The Change Masters</u>. New York: Simon and Schuster.

Katz, D. & Kahn, R. (1978). <u>The Social Psychology of Organizations</u> (2nd Ed.). New York: Wiley.

Katzell, R.A. & Yankelovich, D. (1975). <u>Work Productivity and Job Satisfaction</u>. New York: Psychological Corporation.

Kolodny, H.F. & Kiggundu, M.N. (1980). Towards the Development of a Sociotechnical Systems Model in Woodlands Mechanical Harvesting. <u>Human Relations</u>, <u>33</u>(9), pp. 623-645.

Lee, C. (1990). Beyond Teamwork. <u>Training</u>, <u>27</u>(6), 25-32.

Likert, R. (1961). <u>New Patterns of Management</u>. New York: McGraw-Hill.

Locke, E.A. (1976). The Nature and Causes of Job Satisfaction. In M.D. Dunnette (Ed.), <u>Handbook of Industrial and Organizational Psychology</u> (pp. 297-329. Chicago: Rand McNally.

Marqulies, N. & Colfish, L. (December, 1982). A Sociotechnical Approach To Planning and Implementing New Technology. <u>Training and Development Journal</u>, 16-29.

Maslow, A.H. (1943). A Theory of Human Motivation. <u>Psychological Review</u>, <u>50</u>, 379-396.

McGregor, D.M. (1960). <u>The Human Side of Enterprise</u>. New York: McGraw-Hill.

Mohrman, S.A. & Cummings, T.G. (1989). Self-Designing Organizations. New York: Addison-Wesley.

Morgan, G. (1986). Images of Organizations. Beverly Hills, CA: Sage.

Nadler, D.A. & Tushman, M.L. (1989). Organizational Frame Bending: Principles for Managing Reorientation. The Academy of Management Executives, 3 (3), 194-204.

Norusis, M.J. (1988). SPSS/PC+ Advanced Statistics (Computer program manual). Chicago, IL: SPSS.

Norusis, M.J. (1988). SPSS/PC+ V2.0 Base Manual (Computer program manual). Chicago, IL: SPSS.

Orsburn, J., Moran, L., Musselwhite, E., Zenger, J. (1990). Self-Directed Work Teams: The New American Challenge. San Diego: University Associates.

Parker, Jr., W.S. (1991, June). "Managing and Understanding Resistance to Large Systems Change: A Comprehensive Approach." Paper presented at the Best Practices Seminar, University of Michigan School of Business, Ann Arbor.

Passmore, W.A. (1982, Spring). Overcoming the Roadblocks in Work-Restructuring Efforts. Organizational Dynamics, 54-67.

Passmore, W.A. (1988). Designing Effective Organizations: The Sociotechnical Systems Perspective. New York: John Wiley.

Passmore, W.A., Francis, C., Halderman, J. & Shani, A. (1982). Sociotechnical Systems: A North American Reflection on Empirical Studies of the Seventies. Human Relations, 35 (12), 1179-1204.

Passmore, W.A. & Sherwood, J.J. (1978). Organizations as Sociotechnical Systems. In W.A. Passmore & J.J. Sherwood (Eds.), Sociotechnical Systems: A Sourcebook, (pp. 3-7). La Jolla, CA: University Associates.

Paul, W.J., Robertson, K.B. & Herzberg, F. (1969). Job Enrichment Pays Off. Harvard Business Review, 47, 61-78.

Pava, C. (1983). Managing New Office Technology. New York: The Free Press.Pava, C. (1986).

Redesigning Sociotechnical Systems Design: Concepts and Methods for the 1990's. The Journal of Applied Behavioral Science, 22(3), pp.201-221.

Proctor, B.H. (1986). A Sociotechnical Work-Design System at Digital Enfield: Utilizing Untapped Resources. National Productivity Review, 5(3), 262-270.

Rice, A.K. (1958). Productivity and Social Organization: The Ahmedabad Experiment. London: Tavistock.

Robey, D. (1986). Designing Organizations (2nd Ed.). Homewood, Ill: Irwin.

Roethlisberger, F.J. & Dickson, W.J. (1939). Management and the Worker. Cambridge: Harvard University.

Sabiers, M.P. (1990). Sociotechnical Systems Design Elements: Do They Make A Difference in Organizations? Unpublished manuscript. Case Western Reserve University, Weatherhead School of Management, Cleveland.

Sabiers, M.P. (1992). Generating Critical Organizational States: Bridges Between Sociotechnical Design Features and High Performance. (Doctoral dissertation, Case Western Reserve University, 1991).

Schultheiss, E.E. (1988). Optimizing the Organization: How to Link People and Technology. Cambridge: Bellinger.

Stahl, M.J. & Bounds, G.M. (Eds.). (1991). Competing Globally through Customer Value. New York: Quorum.

Stalk, G. Jr. & Hout, T.M. (1990). Competing Against Time. New York: Free Press.

Sundstrom, E., DeMeuse, K., & Futrell, D. (1990). Work Teams: Applications and Effectiveness. American Psychologist, 45, 120-133.

Tabachnick, B.G. & Fidell, L.S. (1983). Using Multivariate Statistics. San Francisco: Harper & Row.

Taylor, F.W. (1947). The Principles of Scientific Management. New York: Harper & Row.

Taylor, J.C. (1979). Job Design Criteria Twenty Years Later. In L.E. Davis & J.C. Taylor (Eds.), Design of Jobs (2nd Ed.). (pp. 54-63). Santa Monica: Goodyear.

Taylor, J.C. (1989, May). An Action Basis of Social Theory: Looking at the Product of Our Work: A New Paradigm for Designing Effective Organizations. In J. Kubin (Ed.), <u>Dilemmas of Effective Social Action</u> (pp. 1-24). Warsaw, Poland: Polish Academy of sciences.

Trist, E.L. (1979). On Sociotechnical Systems. In W.A. Pasmore & J.J. Sherwood (Eds.), <u>Sociotechnical Systems: A Sourcebook</u> (pp. 43-71). La Jolla, CA: University Associates.

Trist, E.L. (1981). The Sociotechnical Perspective. In A.H. Van de Ven & W.F. Joyce (Eds.), <u>Perspectives on Organization Design and Behavior</u> (pp. 19-75). New York: John Wiley.

Trist, E.L. & Bamforth, K. (1951). Some Social and Psychological Consequences of the Longwall Method of Coal-Getting. <u>Human Relations</u>, <u>4</u>, 3-38.

Turner, A.N. & Lawrence, P.R. (1965). <u>Industrial Jobs and the Worker</u>. Boston: Harvard Graduate School of Business Administration.

Velocci, A.L., Jr. (1991, December). TQM Makes Rocketdyne Tougher Competitor. <u>Aviation Week and Space Technology</u>, 68-69.

Walton, R.E. (1972). How to Counter Alienation in the Plant. <u>Harvard Business Review</u>, 70-81.

Walton, R.E. (1974). Innovative Restructuring of Work. In J.M. Rosow (Ed.), <u>The Worker on the Job: Coping with Change</u> (pp. 145-176). Englewood Cliffs, NJ: Prentice Hall.

Walton, R.E. (1985. From Control to Commitment. <u>Harvard Business Review</u>, 77-84.

Warr, P. & Hall, T. (1979). History of Work Concepts. In L.E. Davis & J.C. Taylor (Eds.), <u>Design of Jobs</u> (2nd Ed.). (pp. 21-28). Santa Monica: Goodyear.

Wellins, R. & George J. (1991). The Key to Self-Directed Teams. <u>Training and Development Journal</u>, <u>45</u>(4),, 26-31.

Zemke, R. (1987). Sociotechnical Systems: Bringing People and Technology Together, <u>24</u> (2), 47-57.

Warrington S. Parker Jr, Ph.D.

Sedona, AZ

ABOUT THE AUTHOR

Warrington S. Parker, Jr. was born in Mobile, Alabama, during the era of Jim Crow laws, which profoundly influenced his sense of and commitment to social justice. After moving to Detroit, Michigan, at an impressionable age, he encountered racism in a more subtle but equally egregious form. These experiences fueled his lifelong dedication to equality and fairness.

Warrington earned his B.A. in Sociology with a minor in Secondary Education from St. Procopius College in Lisle, Illinois (now Benedictine University) and Wayne State University, Detroit, Michigan. His interest in the structure of systems, organizations, communities, and cultures began in college and guided his career trajectory.

After graduating, he taught at his high school alma mater, coaching football and baseball for two years. He then became the head teacher of math and later the Director of Adult and Special Youth Basic Education at the Detroit Public Schools' Skills Training Center, later renamed The McNamara Center. This program, supported by the Manpower Development Training Act (MDTA) passed by President Kennedy, focused on retraining adults and special youth. Warrington played a key role in transforming an old military building into an educational facility.

After three years, he became Director of Community Affairs for the Michigan Catholic Conference, where he focused on community change. He then joined the University of Michigan's Institute for Social Research (ISR) as a Program Associate in Organizational and Community Change while completing his doctoral degree in Organizational Psychology at the University of Michigan, focusing on organizational change.

Warrington also served as an Assistant Professor and Director of Community Affairs at the University of Michigan, School of Management, Dearborn, where he taught Organizational Change, Organizational Development (OD), Organization Design, and Organization Theories to undergraduate and master's level students. He also consulted with the Detroit Public School Superintendent to develop a management training academy for managers and worked with other educational institutions, including the Winchester Neighborhood Private Independent School (WNS) in California.

In 1978, Warrington joined the Rockwell Corporation's Automotive Business in Troy, Michigan, as an Organizational Psychologist, where he served as an internal organizational change agent. His work was featured in several articles, including "The Bold New World of Rockwell" in *Industry Week*, June 1987, and "Leaders of Leaders" in *Patriot's Magazine*. He was also awarded the Peter Drucker Distinguished Speakers Award.

During his time at Rockwell, Warrington lectured in the Republic of China in 1988, addressing government ministers on transitioning to a market-driven economy while maintaining control over production. He also led a successful turnaround of Bellflower Junior/High School in Bellflower, CA, with support from Rockwell and educational consultant Barbara Barnes. For his efforts, he received Rockwell's Citizen Award.

In retirement, Warrington served as Vice President of the International Brain Education Association (IBRA), where he successfully established a Korean NGO at the United Nations in New York. He also organized and spoke at the International Brain Education Conference at the UN and served as Vice President of Research and Development for the Brain Research Institute in South Korea. As Director of Brain Education in the United States, he trained teachers and students.

In 2013, Warrington was invited as Vice President of IBRA to address the Embassy of El Salvador and several African Embassies on Brain Education and its impact on reducing gang violence. He has published numerous articles in *Brain World Magazine* and co-authored "The Brain at School and Work," an unpublished article for teachers at the Academy in Detroit, Michigan.

Warrington and his wife were invited to help turn around the struggling Timbuktu Academy of Science and Technology (now Obama Leadership Academy) in Detroit. After four years, the school received a five-year charter extension. His next book, *A School Turnaround of an African-Centered, Detroit Public Charter School: A Systemic Change Strategy*, will be published in November 2024.

Currently, Warrington serves as the Director and Professor of the Master's Degree Program in the Science of Regenerative Earth Management, an online degree program in Arizona. He now enjoys life at home in Sedona, AZ, where he teaches an online course, "The Science of Regenerative Earth Management," lives on a golf course, practices yoga for strength and flexibility, and writes about his experiences.

Author: *Strength of Will,* published on Amazon, July 2023. Articles published in *Brain World Magazine.*